To the Ends of the Earth

High Plains to Patagonia

I0156502

by

Nelda Bedford Gaydou

RISING PHOENIX PRESS

For my parents, with love and gratitude

Acknowledgments

I would like to thank my brother, David A. Bedford, for all his practical help and encouragement and my niece, Sabrina Bedford, for her delightful artwork.

Table of Contents

PRELUDE – 1944

An Unsettling Letter

"He used often to say there was only one Road; that it was like a great river: its springs were at every doorstep, and every path was its tributary. 'It's a dangerous business, Frodo, going out of your door,' he used to say. 'You step into the Road, and if you don't keep your feet, there is no knowing where you might be swept off to."

—J.R.R. Tolkien, The Lord of the Rings

The road ran straight ahead, a gray ribbon across the greenish-brown ground that spread out tight and flat in every direction—all else was clear blue sky. Only an occasional tumbleweed broke the illusion of a painted landscape.

The day promised to be another scorcher. Benjamin cast a surreptitious glance at his watch, which read 9:30. It was only seventy-five miles to Plainview, and a quick calculation told him that they should arrive in time for an early lunch and have the entire afternoon for enrolling at Wayland Baptist University. He could hardly complain of the Chevy's flat tire that had caused their late start: his own vehicle, a ten-year-old Model B Ford, was barely up to running errands around town and getting him back and forth over the twelve miles between Clovis and Pleasant Hill. It was very good indeed of Gordon Smith to leave his farm for a day to take him. A speck moving toward them caught his attention. As it neared, it revealed itself to be a dusty pickup truck.

"Mailman," said Mr. Smith. Both he and Benjamin raised their hands in greeting as the vehicle drew level with them. But the mail carrier honked his horn and flagged them down.

"Mornin'! I have a letter for Pastor Bedford. Might as well give it to you now." He passed the letter through the window, waved away their thanks, ground into first, and took off.

"It's from Dr. Aulick," said Benjamin. He tore the envelope open, consumed with curiosity. There was a single sheet with a hasty note scribbled on it: "Please see me before you enroll at Wayland." Benjamin read the note out loud.

"What shall we do?" asked Mr. Smith.

"I reckon I ought to see him," sighed Benjamin.

So, instead of turning east at Texico and crossing the state line, they headed west toward Clovis. Benjamin's imagination ran riot as he wondered what Dr. Aulick might possibly want to tell him that couldn't wait until after he had settled things in Plainview. He remembered another time when a broken-down vehicle had meant a drastic change in his family's fortunes.

Vignettes
1932-1944

The Little Model T that Couldn't

The Model T truck was filled to the brim—and then some. There were eleven humans, Fritz the dog, a rabbit and as many personal and household items as could be crammed in: clothing, bedrolls and cooking utensils. The Bedfords were on the move again.

For a cowboy who had waited until he was thirty-two to get married, Benjamin Franklin Bedford was the consummate family man. Circumstances had forced him to change jobs and locations often but, as far as possible, where one Bedford went, they all went. Ben came by his love and knowledge of the land honestly as the son of a Texas Ranger and grandson of a Cherokee chieftain's daughter. He had spent long hours in the saddle ranching and farming, starting at his birthplace, Llano, in the very heart of Texas. By 1900 he had worked his way up into Indian Territory, soon to become part of the new state of Oklahoma. There, sitting at a friend's sickbed, he had met Nancy Tennessee ("Tennie") Anthony, a spirited petite sixteen-year-old with large luminous blue eyes and a tiny waist. A few months later they were married by a Native American pastor and began to raise their family.

Ben's sisters Lucy and Sarah, both of whose husbands were surnamed Phillips though they were not related, lived in the Sulphur Springs Valley of southern Arizona, which had recently opened up for homesteading. The Bedfords decided to accept the challenge of moving with their two small sons, Jonas and Ancil Travis (better known as A.T.), to the frontier area just north of the international border: Douglas, Arizona on the U.S. side and Agua Prieta, Sonora on the Mexican side. The railroad ran through town and served two copper smelters, the prosaically named Calumet and Arizona Company Smelter and the more romantic-sounding Copper Queen. They lived there for nearly fifteen years, and the family grew to include Troy, Lawrence Daniel (L.D.), Billie and Mary. They ranched and farmed, worked in the mines and at one point even ran a small store from their house.

It was a time of unrest due to political upheaval and armed rebellion in nearby Mexico. Revolutionary leader Pancho Villa and his men were in the middle of a prolonged game of cat and mouse with that country's authorities, and there were frequent clashes along the border. Local legend had Pancho Villa riding a horse up the staircase in the Hotel Godsen's lobby in 1912. That year the Ninth Cavalry was sent to Douglas and the Thirteenth Cavalry to El Paso to contain the rebel forces and enforce neutrality, and the Bedfords had a free front-row seat in this particular theater of history. Pancho Villa and his men took advantage of the fact that the Mexican government's forces were reluctant to fire at them over the border, lest they give the United States an excuse to invade Mexico and take yet another chunk of its territory.

Sometimes the whole town turned out to watch these skirmishes. At one of them, Tennie saw a teenage girl jumping up and down on a box, cheering the rebels on at the top of her lungs. It was apparent that this greatly annoyed a stiff, dignified-looking older gentleman standing nearby. Finally he could bear it no longer: during one of her more exuberant jumps he kicked the box away and the girl tumbled down in a flurry of arms and legs. But Tennie had closer encounters than that with the famous Pancho Villa and his rebels. One day she stepped out the back door of her house and her heart nearly stopped as dozens of armed men and their horses made their way toward her through the fields. But the General put her mind at rest: "Don't worry, *Señora*. We just need to water our horses and we'll go," and he was as good as his word. On another occasion she came across one of the rebel commanders as she was running an errand on horseback. Tennie, now in her twenties, had become a beautiful woman. He showered her with flowery compliments and melting Latin looks as he rode beside her. Fortunately, he proved to be as gallant as he was eloquent, and allowed her to gallop away at full speed.

A prolonged statewide drought forced the family to seek a change. They moved to Weleetka, in central Oklahoma, where Jonas landed a job with the railroad. They lived there some eight years, a grueling and heartbreaking time. The family shrank and expanded: twin girls Pearl and Muriel were born only to live a few hours. A year and a half later they were followed by a healthy sister, Jewel, and Tennie was pregnant yet again when her fine, handsome firstborn who had never been anything but a source of pride and joy, suddenly fell ill and died. Ardell ("Ira") Paul was born four months later.

The oldest of the remaining siblings took over Jonas' job with the railroad and the family followed him for a short-term assignment in Belen, a small town in central New Mexico whose railroad junction was to earn it the name of "The Hub City." It was there that the eleventh and last of the Bedfords was born: Allen Benjamin. He weighed less than two pounds and was so tiny that his mother pinned his clothes to a pillow for easier handling. Tennie had a nephew with a Hispanic mother-in-law who was thrilled by Benji's dark hair to such an extent that she offered to pay one thousand dollars for him, and Tennie had the feeling she wasn't kidding. But Benji remained at home; his dark hair soon fell out and was replaced by fair silken locks with which his sisters were later to practice hairdressing.

During their brief return to Oklahoma, when Benji was almost two, he somehow tumbled out of a moving wagon and, before L.D. could stop it, the front and back wheels had run over both of his brother's feet. When he was taken for medical attention, the little boy showed his pain and displeasure by pulling the doctor's hair with all his might, but no special treatment was given, and from then on he often required special shoes and wore down their heels unevenly. A few months later, now in Clovis, New Mexico, Benji treated the family to another dose of drama by playing on a windowsill and falling out. Fortunately for him, his oldest sister happened to be outside and proved to have lightning reflexes, catching him in mid-flight.

The job market in Clovis was no better than anywhere else and, other than A.T., Billie was the only one in the family who was able to find a steady job, at $8.00 per week, testing cream and plucking chickens. However, they did have an extended Anthony family support network. Tennie's brothers Ignatius and Crawford, and sister Arizona (married to Ben's widowed brother Seth) both lived there. Their mother, the stern half-Choctaw widow of a Civil War veteran, spent half of her time with "Naysh" and the other half with her son Henry in Oklahoma. When Grandmother Anthony was in town, she always asked for one of her granddaughters to spend the night with her.

The relatives saw each other frequently. Benji decided he was big enough to sleep over at Uncle Naysh and Aunt Maude's house and got permission to do so one night, but by bedtime he was feeling decidedly homesick. Aunt Maude would have none of this wishy-washiness: she gave him a smart spat and marched him off to bed with a "You wanted to spend the night—well, now you are going to spend the night!" In addition to the aunts and uncles and grandmother, there were also cousins and relations by marriage. This abundance of relatives could be a source of confusion. When A.T.'s wife Geneva had Benji go the store for a pack of cigarettes, the merchant hesitated before handing them over to such a small child, and asked who they were for.

"My daughter-in-law," replied Benji matter-of-factly.

Like their neighbors, the Bedfords had been riding the rollercoaster of the High Plains' economy their entire lives. Periods of good rainfall in the late 1800s had attracted large numbers of settlers to the area. Then came the droughts, causing economic recessions and turning the fields into deserts that received the highly descriptive name of "dust bowls." This cycle repeated itself several times into the early 1900s. But the worst Dust Bowl of all coincided with the Great Depression, also known as "The Dirty Thirties." National and personal situations were desperate.

By 1932 the only capital remaining to Ben Bedford consisted of his wits, his will and his faith. Here he was, having to start all over again at sixty-four years of age. He had heard that there was cotton to be picked in Paducah, just south of the Texas Panhandle, at the so-called "Crossroads of America," the intersection of U.S. Highways 70 and 83. Ben borrowed ninety dollars from Grandmother Anthony, bought an old Model T truck, loaded it up and set out for Paducah.

Born to the saddle and skilled at handling horse-drawn carts and ploughs, Ben had never learned to drive a motor vehicle, so his sons Troy and L.D. took turns at the wheel. They left Clovis just before noon and covered the one hundred miles to Lubbock in about six hours. Ben entertained Ira and Benji by singing cowboy songs like "The Old Chisholm Trail" and "Get Along, Little Dogies." He also dazzled them by peeling pecans with a sharp pocket knife, leaving the nut intact. Meanwhile, Mary and Jewel carried on a desultory conversation with their mother.

The canvas they had spread out over the top to protect them from the blazing sun and the slats on the sides of the truck bed prevented them from seeing much of the countryside. But then again, there wasn't much to see. All one hundred miles looked remarkably the same: flat as a pancake, with here and there a farm house flanked by a few lonely trees. As dusk fell, they stopped at some grounds that were later to become part of the Texas Tech University campus, where they spread out groundcovers and bedrolls under the stars. Puzzled by the darkness, L.D.'s little girl Lou piped up: "Somebody turn on the lights!"

In the morning, they loaded everything back into the truck and climbed in. It was L.D.'s turn to drive. His wife, their two girls and Troy were in the cab; the rest were all in the back. Today the view was another story. They were coming down off the high level land of the Llano Estacado into the red beds of the Rolling Plains. The vegetation gradually added scrubby juniper-mesquite woodlands to the prairie grasses, and signs of the age-long work of the Blanco River began to appear: the colorful ditches and gullies of the Caprock Escarpment and the Blanco Canyon.

The road through this fascinating landscape wound up and down increasingly steep hills. Inevitably, it became too much for the long-suffering Model T. Just as they were nearing the top of a particularly sharp rise, about thirty miles east of Lubbock, the transmission went out, and the truck started rolling back down, gathering speed with every passing second. L.D. did the only thing possible—he turned into a bank on the right side of the road, coming to an abrupt, crunching halt that nevertheless avoided major injuries. True, the rabbit escaped in the ensuing confusion, but it was quickly retrieved thanks to Fritz's canine prowess. He had learned to keep his teeth to himself after being beaten with one of the family rabbits that he had killed and was preparing to consume.

The family had five dollars all told, which they were forced to spend on getting the truck pulled out of the ditch. Taking stock of the situation, the older brothers figured that if everyone except the driver walked, the Model T just might be able to make it over the hill. As the family walked and watched, Troy got behind the wheel and started back up the hill. Once again, the truck made it nearly all the way up before faltering and starting back down. Troy knew there would be no way to get it out of the ditch again, so he kept going down, doing his best to stay on the road. The truck finally came to rest at the very brink of a deep gully and refused to start up again.

There they were: eleven persons and a broken-down vehicle in the middle of nowhere, with no money, no job and no idea what to do next. Finally two young men, who were breaking in a truck stripped down to nothing but the chassis and a seat for the driver and a passenger, stopped to see if they could help, their chivalry probably aroused by the sight of the Bedford females. Be that as it may, L.D. decided to approach them and try to arrange to have the Model T towed to Dickens, about thirty miles further east. The only item of value he had to offer was his pistol, which he was wearing. He walked over to the two young men and pulled out the gun.

"Could we get you to pull the truck into Dickens for us?"

"Of course!" stammered one of the young men. "Anything you say!"

"No, no, you misunderstand me," L.D. hastened to explain. "The only thing I can pay you with is this gun."

The young men agreed to tow the truck with everybody and everything in it all the way to Dickens. They stopped at a campground outside of town and parked the disabled vehicle. While the family got down and stretched out, Ben strode resolutely to the general store in Dickens with empty hands and empty pockets.

He was gone for quite a while, but when he returned he brought groceries, cotton sacks, a job and a place to live. He had met a local land owner and struck an agreement to harvest the cotton crop. The next day the farmer arrived at the campground with a team of horses and pulled the old truck to his place, where it remained until it was forgotten, along with the plan to go to Paducah.

Sharecropping

At harvest time everyone pitched in. For that first crop, they all had bags to fill with cotton—there was even a special small one for five-year-old Benji. He was teamed with Troy who, aware that his little brother loved to make a good showing when the sacks were weighed, would pull cotton and lay it between the rows for him to stuff in his sack when he began to fall behind. Benji soon acquired useful new skills. When they used the sled cutter, it was his job to drive the two horses in a straight line so that the sharp blades protruding at ninety-degree angles on either side would scythe through the plants. As they went down the furrows, the first men would snatch armfuls of the crop and drop them on the ground. The next in line would form bundles, bind them and stack them. After that he mastered the cultivator. It had two large metal wheels that looked as if they belonged to an oversized bicycle. A skimpy bare frame was held together by metal rods and, perched high on a bright orange seat in the middle, Benji could control the action of the blades by pulling a lever on the side while he drove the team of four horses or mules that drew it.

The Bedfords poured their energies into sharecropping near the town of Dickens, starting at the Stevens' place, which came with a small two-bedroom house. After a season there they moved on to the Gilstrap site for a couple of years before finally settling down in the Reynolds' place, near Croton.

Odd jobs were a welcome source of extra income, and the family took on just about anything. On one occasion Ben dug a well and was given a mare and a colt in exchange. Except for the mare, which was soon sold to cover expenses, and the colt, which became the younger boys' pet, the farm animals belonged to the farmer, but the Bedfords could use them and were responsible for their care.

Ira and Benji once helped clear a field of mesquite stumps and roots, a process known as grubbing. The stumps were theirs to keep, and the family used them for fuel. The boys wore dark blue felt hats that someone had given them in Clovis as protection against the sun. One day they had the help, or at least the company, of Troy's future stepsons, Burton and Tom, who were about the same age as the youngest Bedfords. While Ben drove them home, the boys entertained themselves by snatching Benji's hat off his head and tossing it on the ground, forcing him to hop on and off the wagon over and over. Finally Benji decided to take countermeasures. As they reached for the hat one more time, Benji grabbed the rim and held on for dear life, but they already had a good grip and tugged. The crown flew off, leaving the rim firmly hugging Benji's head. So ended the little blue felt hat, amid gales of laughter.

There was also plenty to do indoors. There was no electricity, no gas, no running water and no sewer system. Water, that precious commodity, had to be taken from the ground, either manually with a hand pump or with a windmill. It flowed into a large round barrel where fruit jars filled with foodstuffs that needed to be kept cool were placed: milk, butter, cream and meat. The overflow went into the trough to water the animals.

Monday was the usual laundry day. A popular ditty that little girls sang at that time ran: "Monday is wash day at our house; we're happy as can be. I wash clothes for my dolly, while Mommy scrubs for me!" The reality was not quite that light-hearted. A large heavy iron tub was set on supports. Water had to be carted from the well to fill it and fires lit underneath to make the water boil. White clothes and linens were washed first; they were usually rinsed twice in big zinc tubs, the last time with bluing. The order in which the remaining clothes were washed depended on how soiled they were: work clothes came last because they were the dirtiest. After being boiled to loosen the dirt, they were vigorously scrubbed on wooden washboards with metal ridges, using soap made at home from lard. Clothes that required starching were dipped into a starch solution and hung on the line to dry. Ironing usually took place the next day. The clothes were sprinkled with water and rolled up to dampen evenly. Meanwhile, the flat iron was heated on the cook stove or over an open fire. Everything was ironed, except underwear and socks.

Another day which required hauling large amounts of water was Saturday, the usual day for bathing by immersion. Round galvanized tubs large enough to sit in were partially filled with cold water and brought to bathing temperature with kettles of boiling water. Afterwards, the dirty water had to be hauled back outside because there were no drains.

Since there was no running water, there were no indoor toilets. A hole was dug and an outhouse built over it some distance from the house. Catalogues from Sears Roebuck Co. and Montgomery Ward did double duty as reading and cleaning material. Washed and dried corn cobs were also used in lieu of toilet paper. A bag of white "lime" powder (usually calcium hypochlorite) was kept nearby and a scoopful was added to the hole periodically to kill the odor and bacteria. It did such a good job of this that the waste did not get broken down and the hole eventually filled up. At that point, a new hole would have to be dug nearby. The dirt from the new pit would be placed on top of the old one, and the outhouse would be moved over the new hole.

Extra digging was required at the Gilstrap place because there was no storm cellar. Cellars were essential, for they provided shelter during violent storms and tornadoes, as well as storage space for canned goods. Fruit and vegetables were planted in abundance in the kitchen garden. Everything that was not eaten fresh was "canned" for the winter months in large glass jars. When animals were killed for food, whatever could not be eaten right away was also cooked and canned. In winter, sides of beef or pork were often hung out by the windmill, where they would freeze. Pork was sometimes salted, and bacon and sausage were staples of the country diet. At the table, Troy would solemnly say, "Pass us the strawberries and steaks, please," as his plate was heaped with red beans and pork.

Daily chores included feeding and milking the cows. There was butter to be churned; the chickens had to be fed and the eggs gathered. The wood-burning cook stove required regular stoking, especially in winter. It could be quite temperamental and often flared up. One morning the younger children were outside waiting for the school bus when they saw black smoke rolling out of the chimney, so they raced back to help put out the fire. But the most memorable occasion was the day that the stove caught fire while

Tennie was preparing breakfast. She had just cut out the biscuits when fire broke out. She dropped the pan on the floor and, in the ensuing confusion, forgot all about it and stepped in the middle of the biscuits with her bare feet. When things were safely under control she calmly picked up the pan and slid the biscuits into the oven. She wasn't about to let that good food go to waste, although the biscuits did have a peculiar shape that day.

The family had several kerosene lamps, but the best lighting came from the Aladdin lamp, whose use had become widespread by the early 1930s. It had a round wick that provided an even, non-flickering blue flame, burning with virtually one hundred percent fuel efficiency; average consumption was around fifty hours of service per gallon of kerosene. The lamp was equipped with a rare-earth oxide mantle that glowed incandescently, producing the same amount of white light as a sixty-watt light bulb. The difference with the other lamps was so great that the Aladdin Company offered a one thousand dollar reward to any person who could show an oil lamp with equal illumination. The reward was never collected.

Since money was so scarce, everything possible was grown or prepared at home. Store-bought items were limited to things like flour, cornmeal, sugar, salt and baking powder (when the starter dough wasn't enough). Many of these products came in twenty-five or fifty-pound cotton bags. Around 1925 the sacks began to appear in different colors when it became clear that the sacks themselves were sought after as sewing material and were a splendid marketing tool. Hard-to-wash-out stamps were replaced by easy-to-detach paper labels. By the late 1930s there was heated competition to offer the most attractive prints as the brands consumers bought depended increasingly on the desirability of the sacks. Some even carried pre-printed patterns for dresses, dolls, stuffed animals, appliqués and quilt blocks. To economize on footwear, rubber half soles could be bought to repair worn-down shoes, but when money was too tight for that, cardboard did the trick.

Of course there were treats that did not require practically any money, and ice cream was at the top of the list, since it was delicious and the only bought items it required were ice and salt. Most households had iceboxes, some of which were very handsome pieces of furniture, usually made of wood and standing on legs. They had hollow walls lined with tin or zinc and packed with insulating materials such as cork, sawdust, straw or seaweed. A large block of ice was fed from the top into a tray or compartment, and cold air circulated down and around the rest of the storage area, which was equipped with shelves. Items were inserted and removed through doors on the front. The fancier models had spigots for draining the ice water from a catch pan or holding tank, while the simpler models required placing drip pans underneath that had to be emptied at least once per day.

Originally ice was harvested in winter from snow-packed areas or frozen lakes and stored in icehouses to await delivery. But natural sources were easily contaminated and, when mechanical refrigerators were invented, they were installed in large industrial plants that produced ice for home delivery, door to door, first in horse-drawn wagons and later in motor vehicles. In and around Dickens, the iceman drove a blue pickup. He wore a leather apron and slung a sack over his shoulder to protect it from the blocks of ice he heaved from the icehouse to his truck and from there to his customers' iceboxes. His tools were wires, hooks, tongs and icepicks. Most households took one fourth of a block, and the iceman could mark and split the blocks with wonderful precision. He could always use help on his deliveries, and Benji sometimes earned extra pennies or was paid with ice for assisting him.

The ice cream maker consisted of a tall wooden ice bucket, permanently kept moist to prevent cracking. It was equipped with a handle for rotating the metal container and the paddle that stirred the mixture. Ben loved ice cream and was in charge of the entire process. Benji would sit by his father throughout the procedure and help "clean" the paddle. Vanilla was the staple, but the flavor could be varied according to the fruit on hand and, as an extra-special treat, there was chocolate. Sometimes Tennie would bake a cake to go along with it. The whole family would gather and often neighbors were invited to help polish off the batch while they relaxed and talked and laughed together. This quality time was a well-established family tradition, and the older children could remember their father spending long hours cranking the handle of the ice cream bucket and talking over passages from the Bible with his brother-in-law Henry in Oklahoma.

As things stabilized, Benji's older siblings began finding their own niches. While the rest of the family was at the "big house" on the Reynolds' place, L.D. and Billie lived in the "little house" with their daughters. One day Lou, who was two or three years younger than Benji, had picked and eaten some green fruit. Tennie gave her a spat and sent her home. When her parents asked where she had been spanked, she sobbed, "Between the houses!" Eventually they branched out on their own, first at Spur and later on in Odessa.

Mary moved back to Clovis and began dating Carl Beck. Meanwhile Billie, who had been in Clovis all along, married Marion Alexander and helped him build up a trucking business and establish a wholesale-retail market, while Troy was content to remain at home for now. A.T. definitely had the most colorful employment history. The railroad job he had inherited when Jonas died took him as far away as Peru for a time. At the height of the Depression A.T. worked in Clovis for the Works Progress Administration (WPA), a program for the unemployed created under President Franklin D. Roosevelt's New Deal. Whenever he could, he sent money to help the family. At one point A.T. spent a year with them in Dickens, working on the farm. Before planting, he asked the farmer how deep he wanted the seeds placed in the ground. The farmer answered, "Oh, about a thumb's length."

When it was time for the seeds to sprout, the farmer was puzzled: "How far down did you plant them things?!"

"A thumb's length, just like you said," replied A.T., stretching out his hands. All became clear: A.T.'s huge, work-roughened hands and fingers were twice as large as the farmer's!

Vinegar, Vinegar

"Three geese flying south with old Southall in their mouths; when they found they had a fool, they dropped him off at Patton Springs Grammar School," ran a doggerel with which the local children poked fun at their principal. The Patton Springs School was located in Afton, north of Dickens, and gathered the children not only from town but from the surrounding rural area as well. Jewel, Ira and Benji went to this school after they moved to the Reynolds' place in Croton. Of their older siblings, only L.D. had graduated from high school. Neither of their parents had completed grade school, but they were great readers and Ben was famous for his beautiful penmanship.

Patton Springs was the latest in the string of schools Jewel and Ira had attended, but it was only the second for Benji. His first was in Dickens. He was all expectation as the bus picked them up for his first day of school. It was January, the middle of the school year, because he had had to stay home to help bring in the crops during the first semester. Benji climbed on and sat down beside a neighbor, a little red-haired girl whose father ranched the land just behind the Stevens' place. An older boy started making fun of him, but before Benji could decide on his response, the little red-haired girl swung her lunch-pail around and slammed it into the side of his tormentor's head. There was no more bullying on the school bus. However, he did get a good laugh out of his classmates later that day. When the bell rang, he dashed to his locker and grabbed his lunch-pail, only to be told, amid peals of laughter, that it was just morning recess. Lunch usually consisted of home-made biscuits with thick slices of sausage. The yearly school picnic, with store-bought white bread and baloney, was a citified culinary delight for them.

When the school performed eye exams on the children, Benji was found to have a slight deficiency. "Do you think your mother would want you to wear glasses, sonny?" asked the examiner. "No!" replied Benji, and never breathed a word about it at home.

But Benji was by no means unprepared for school. He was already well advanced in two of the three "Rs". He loved stories and Ira would read to him, often in exchange for a chore he didn't want to do, while Benji kept careful tabs ("You still owe me two stories!"). At some point the print Ira read resolved into words that Benji could recognize for himself. His "rithmatic" grew out of a passion for keeping track of the rows and furrows, stacks and bags completed by each family member as they harvested the crops, and he already had a proven track record in problem solving. When they were still in Clovis and Benji was no more than four or five years old, he and Ira had been enjoying the forbidden pleasures of playing on the tracks of a railroad bridge when a truck miscalculated the clearance space beneath it and became tightly wedged. The boys looked and listened as the men reached the conclusion that they would have to take the truck apart to get it out. Benji gave the driver a disgusted look: "Why don't you just let the air out of the tires, Mister?" Sure enough, that did the trick.

Writing was the only "R" that gave him any trouble, probably because he, like Scout Finch in *To Kill a Mockingbird*, landed in an experimental program that consisted of flashing cards at random while the class "received these impressionistic revelations in silence." Forever after he knew the letters that went in every word, but when he wrote them down, they did not necessarily come out in the proper order. Unfortunately, he did not inherit his father's beautiful penmanship and his handwriting was truly frightful.

Although Benji was bumped up from Lower to Upper First, he still got out earlier than his brother and sister, and usually spent the time socializing with his new friends. Often they would play marbles, a game at which Benji could definitely hold his own. Sometimes they played for keeps, and on one such occasion he had won twenty marbles from his classmates and was working on recovering an "agate," his favorite starter marble, now in the hands of a rival. Ira caught up with him at this point and made him return all the marbles he had won. He not only lost the twenty new ones, but his trusty old agate as well.

Benji was the one commissioned to pick up items from the store while he was waiting for his siblings. No money changed hands because the grocer kept a running account of the family's purchases in that precursor of the credit card, the trusty old handwritten notebook, and the balance was paid monthly. One afternoon Benji had a special errand to run for his mother. She had asked him to get vinegar because they were having company and she wanted to make a vinegar pie. After picking it up, he returned to the school and, while they were waiting for the upper grades to be let out, he entertained his friends by imitating their teacher. At a lively point in his performance he dropped the quart glass jug, which shattered on the ground. Desperate, he had his brother called out of class for a consult.

"Just go get another jug and don't say anything about it. I won't tell."

Benji followed his advice. This unconfessed sin haunted his conscience and gave Ira ideal grounds for blackmail for a long time. Whenever he wanted to make a stubborn Benji give in or do a chore that he himself disliked, he would simply murmur "Vinegar, vinegar," and Benji would fall into line, unaware that his mother had known about the two jugs of vinegar as soon as she had settled her monthly bill and hadn't given the matter a second thought.

Bottle Ranch

"Bottle Ranch" was an elaborate game the younger boys had developed when they lived in Clovis. Slender bottles were horses, fat bottles were cows and small round jars were sheep and goats. Labels peeled off of cans served as currency: the smaller the paper, the larger the denomination. One enterprising friend had converted a cigarette roller into a miniature baler to prepare grass "hay" for the horses. After they moved they only had each other to play with, but once they started going to school they began making new friends. However, their social life began to revolve increasingly around church.

Ben and Tennie had been members of a Free Will Baptist Church in Oklahoma, but their attendance had been somewhat erratic of late because of their frequent moves. Whenever they could, they would walk or ride a wagon to the nearest church. Ira recalled going to a revival meeting at the Brethren Church on West Seventh Street in Clovis, near the La Casita School which the school-aged Bedfords attended. A pastor by the name of Weeks had preached and, when he was greeting the people after the service was over, had laid his hand on four-year-old Benji's head as he told his father, "This boy is going to be a preacher and serve in many different missions." But all that Benji remembered about it was the baptisms that took place in a big metal tank and an invitation that tugged strangely at something inside him, starting a struggle that he put up every Sunday until he was eight.

When they lived at the Gilstrap place, the nearest place of worship was Midway Baptist Church, half-way between Dickens and Afton as its name suggested, but it was still quite a long walk, so that it was usually only Ira and Benji who went with their father. But Friendship Baptist Church in Croton was only a mile and a half by road and three-fourths of a mile across the fields from the Reynolds' place. There was a part-time pastor, Jess Terry, who went to Croton twice a month. On those weekends, he would preach on Saturday night and Sunday morning. However, there was an activity for the young people every Saturday night and Sunday School every Sunday morning.

The older siblings opted to stay at home, while Jewel continued her practice of rotating between the services of the Midway Baptist, Methodist and Church of Christ congregations to which her three best friends belonged, thereby broadening her social base considerably. But Ben, Tennie, Ira and Benji attended Friendship regularly, at times on foot and at others in a two-horse wagon. Mrs. Butler was the boys' Sunday School teacher. She loved children and came up with all sorts of ways to keep them interested and motivated. Benji's very first Bible was a New Testament with a felt cover that Mrs. Butler gave him for reading and memorizing a certain number of verses.

There were frequent pie suppers when the church families would get together to socialize. Croton itself didn't have much more than a grocery store, a filling station and the church But there was a windmill and an earthen water tank that the children used for swimming in the summer and the church used for baptisms when the occasion arose. The children would usually gather at the home of one of the church families to play on Sunday afternoon. Sometimes they would hold their own rodeos, roping and riding calves and young horses. Ira got wind of Benji's accepting a dare to ride an unbroken colt for one of these performances and issued a firm veto.

One Sunday morning Tennie said, "Ben, we really should have the pastor over for lunch." She was a bit taken aback when her husband brought him home that very day. It was the first of many shared lunches over which their friendship deepened. When Benji had to have his tonsils removed, it was Pastor Terry who drove him to the drugstore in Farwell, where he got a ride on into Clovis. And it was Jess Terry who baptized nine-year-old Benji in the water tank, after a decision made during a revival, when Ira overhead the following exchange between two of the older church members:

"That wasn't much of a response—just one junior boy for baptism."

"That's what they said when George W. Truett[1] was converted and look what happened. Who knows what this boy might become?"

---

[1] One of the most influential Southern Baptists of his time. He began life on a small farm in North Carolina and eventually became pastor of the First Baptist Church in Dallas and President of the Southern Baptist Convention. President Woodrow Wilson invited him to address the Allied troops in Europe during World War I, and he gave a famous speech on freedom of religion on the steps of the U.S. Capitol Building.

Odd Jobs

Things finally seemed to be looking up for the Bedfords after three hard years of work in Texas. They had even bought a Model A Ford that Troy drove, while Ben stuck with the wagon. But one night in December Ben starting coughing up blood and couldn't stop. Troy rushed him to L.D.'s house in Spur, where he could get medical attention, but it was too late: he was in the final stage of tuberculosis. Troy returned for the children and sent for the older sisters in Clovis, Billie and Mary, who along with Troy's future wife Sue, rushed to their father's side in Spur.

The family crowded into the house and the children were sent to sleep on pallets on the floor. During the night Sue woke them and called them to the bedside. There, surrounded by the family he loved, Ben Bedford passed away at the age of sixty-seven. He was buried in Spur, next to his baby granddaughter's grave, which was marked only by the rough tombstone L.D. had carved himself because he had had no money to buy one. Pastor Terry held the funeral.

Widowed at forty-nine, Tennie remained at the Reynolds place another year and a half to fulfill the obligations of the sharecropping agreement. Troy married Sue and moved to Clovis, but he and other men from the extended family returned periodically to help his mother and the boys bring in the crops. Tennie took thirteen-year-old Ira aside and told him, "You're the oldest boy left at home now, so you will have to be the man of the family. You must learn to drive."

So Troy gave Ira driving lessons. His previous experience behind the wheel had not been promising. A few months earlier Troy had been working on a minor mechanical problem with the car and needed someone to sit behind the wheel and let the clutch in to get the motor started while he pushed. He quickly explained to Ira about the gears, the clutch and the accelerator: "It's very simple. I just need to get the motor started and then I'll take over." Unfortunately, the motor roared into life at the very first touch and the car took off at such a speed that Troy was unable to jump onto the sideboard in time. The car was moving purposefully toward the road and Ira didn't know how to control or stop it. At the last moment he instinctively pulled at the wheel, avoiding the road, and eventually came to a halt with no further mishap.

Now Ira sat tensely behind the wheel, determined to do his duty. Benji sat in the back seat and audited the lessons, unwilling to miss out on anything. Ira's nerves translated into stiff, jerky movements, grinding gear shifts, and abrupt starts and stops before he mastered the art of driving. Much to his chagrin, when nine-year-old Benji managed to wheedle a turn, the car glided effortlessly from one gear to another and purred like a kitten.

Ira was very responsible and conscientious, a born big brother. On one occasion he and Benji had to take the car to Spur for repairs. Benji was all for staying in town and going to the movies while they had the chance.

"People always come up from Croton on Saturday and we can hitch a ride back."

"No, we can't! We have to go home."

So they started walking. After a while a neighbor family passed them going to Spur and, by the time they overtook them again on the way back, the brothers had covered about ten miles. They stopped and offered to take the boys to Croton. To Benji's relief, Ira's conscience was fine with that. They rode as far as the neighbors' house and finished the last two miles on foot.

Tennie traded the Model A for a Ford V-8 whose front-door hinges were in the middle of the car so that they opened out at the front. They rode this car to spend Christmas with L.D. and his family, who now lived in Odessa, where he worked hauling mud for the oil company. Over the holidays Ira and Benji made friends with the Allison boys next door. They lent them their bikes, and Benji learned to ride that Christmas. Although he fell and got quite a lump on his head in the process, he voted it well worthwhile.

By mid-1937 Tennie was through with her obligations in Texas and ready to join the rest of the family in New Mexico. She timed the move to coincide with the beginning of the green bean harvest. Ira and Betty the cow stayed in Clovis with Billie so that Ira, now in junior high school, would not have his studies disrupted. Tennie, Jewel and Benji joined him after several weeks in Portales picking green beans. Benji began the school year in Portales and later transferred to the La Casita Grade School. So, shortly before he turned eleven, Benji settled into the Clovis public school system in the sixth grade.

Benji soon got used to living in town. They rented several different houses, all of which had electricity and bathrooms. His very first tub bath with running water was at Billie's house shortly after their return. When he had been splashing around in there for a good while, she cracked open the door and asked, "Is everything all right in there?"

"Yes," he bellowed. "Go away!"

When they lived on Prince Street, they were at number 312, while Troy and Sue were across the street on the next block, at 409. One day L.D. and his family came for a visit, so the boys slept on the floor. It had rained hard during the day and there was water standing in the ditches. Late that night Sue heard a knock and discovered a sleepwalking Benji on her doorstep. He had effortlessly sailed over the two overflowing ditches, something he had not yet mastered when he was awake. She put him to bed and sent him home early the next morning before his absence was discovered and the family wondered what had become of him.

There were all kinds of odd jobs available and Benji, like the others, took whatever came his way to help with the family economy. Tennie cleaned houses when she could get the work, and the high school found Ira a job he could do in the early morning so he could play on the football team. On weekdays Benji went from house to house distributing a local free-press publication consisting mostly of advertising, and on weekends he hawked the *Denver Post*, the most widely read newspaper in Clovis along with the *Los Angeles Examiner*. When he tried to sell the paper to one local businessman, he was told, "Sonny, I don't want no newspaper. But come back in a few years and I'll give you a job selling cars!"

Troy drove trucks and hauled all sorts of merchandise. Sometimes Benji would help sell the vegetables and fruit he brought back, door to door. He also learned all about checking the soundness of eggs by illuminating them from behind with a strong light, a process called "candling" because it had originally been done by candlelight. Troy's stepsons, Burton and Tommy, had been caddying for some time and now Benji joined them. All they had to do was show up at the golf course after school and on weekends when the weather was good and wait for someone to request their services. There was a banker who always asked for Benji on Saturdays and, although he didn't tip, he played five rounds, which meant a sure $1.25 for the family kitty. The boys even went to a golf tournament in Roswell one weekend. Since there was bound to be a need for caddies, they camped out under the stars on the golf course to be on hand when the action began. Eventually Benji got together a basic set of four clubs: a putter, a nine-iron, a four-iron and a three-wood. He and Tommy would hit the golf balls they found all the way from home to the golf course and, since caddies were allowed to play on the grounds on Saturdays, they soon turned into quite good amateur golfers.

Some odd jobs were paid in kind, rather than cash. On many Saturdays, Benji and Tommy or another one of his friends would sit at a table in front of the movie house and pass out flyers advertising the current offerings to passers-by. In return they were given tickets to the show. They were thus able to keep up with the latest films starring Bob Steele, Tom Nix, John Wayne and Gene Autry.

Billie and Marion owned and operated a wholesale and retail market. When they needed an extra pair of hands, Benji would get called in to fetch and carry, stock shelves and even man the cash register. Marion's brother was the local distributor for Dr. Pepper and sometimes had Benji help deliver bottles and pick up the empty containers. Benjamin's school friend Leonard Lane helped him get a steady part-time job at the local Safeway on Saturdays and sometimes on Fridays after school, where his tasks included carrying bags and stocking shelves. In fact, Benjamin's very first Social Security card included that supermarket chain's name.

Graduation and Ordination

By the time Benjamin graduated from junior high with an award for citizenship, he had grown into the full version of his name and quite a few changes had taken place in the family. He and Tennie had settled down in a small house on Wallace Street because now it was just the two of them. Mary and Jewel had both married and moved to California. Ira had finished high school and had also gone to the West Coast to work for a year before joining the army, rather than waiting to be drafted. They had lost Troy to tuberculosis, and Jess Terry had made a special trip to preach at his funeral. Eventually A.T. married the widow and brought up his brother's daughter Frankie as his own.

And, of course, Billie and Marion had long lived independently. When Benjamin was thirteen or fourteen years old, Marion asked him to work for them on a regular basis, so he resigned from Safeway, dropped his odd jobs and began working for Marion after school on weekdays, from 4:00 to 8:00 p.m., and all day Saturday, from 7:00 a.m. to 11:00 p.m. Twice a week he would ride the truck that made the rounds of the nearby towns (Melrose, Ft. Sumner, St. Vrain) to make deliveries and bring back produce. Many of the neighboring farmers traded dairy products or eggs for merchandise. Billie ran the office and kept tabs of their accounts in her own handwritten notebook. She knew all of the people from Clovis and the surrounding towns, and she would often extend their credit or give them extra fruit and vegetables when they were in especially straitened circumstances. On the remaining days Benjamin would fill in wherever he was needed at the market and make local deliveries in Marion's pickup truck. He was fourteen when he got his first driver's license, and his mother had to authorize it.

Meanwhile Benjamin did his best to keep up with his schoolwork. He was assigned a good number of classics to read for his English class, and more than once books like *A Tale of Two Cities* ended up serving as pillows at night. He was on the debate team, participated in the school play and was elected President of the Student Council during his senior year. And yet, just as it had happened when he was a little boy living in the country, his social life and the activities he was most interested in increasingly revolved around the church.

The Bedfords began attending the First Baptist Church of Clovis soon after their arrival. A short time later the church called a new pastor, J.T. Barbee, whose wife devoted much of her time and energies to the young people. Their daughter was Benjamin's age and they advanced through the Junior and Intermediate Departments together. In fact, she dated both of his best friends, first Walter Hyde and later Leonard Lane.

Even though Sunday was lucrative for caddying, Benjamin felt that he shouldn't work that day and devoted it to church activities. And there were plenty of them. The First Baptist Church had a policy of encouraging young people, training them and giving them opportunities to participate. As a result, a vigorous and creative youth group was born that yielded an outstanding crop of pastors and missionaries. Some of the young people formed a volunteer group that took turns getting together in the homes of the various members. A meeting was held at Benjamin's house that eventually led to a successful campaign and special election to keep liquor out of Clovis.

Every fifth Sunday evening the Training Union would have a special emphasis on missions, and participants were encouraged to come up with new and interesting ways of presenting the material. One Sunday Benjamin and his friends were in charge. Walter, the future engineer, rigged a radio in the church building and they gave a broadcast, with Leonard as announcer and Benjamin as speaker. They later found out that a local radio station had notified the police of airwave interference from an unknown source that night.

At that time New Mexico was the proving grounds for the Southern Baptist Sunday School Board. New materials and methods were tried out there first and later taught at the Seminary. Benjamin was soon teaching a class in his own Intermediate Department and, at the request of the Director, J.T. Harrell, was named his Associate and went visiting with him. Another innovative program to which Benjamin and his friends belonged was the Junior Deacons. There they learned what deacons did and shared in many of their tasks: ushering, taking up the offering, serving the Lord's Supper, visiting, presiding at meetings and even speaking at the Wednesday night prayer meetings and Bible studies.

The Church started a Spanish-language mission that just happened to meet on Sunday afternoons at the pink house that the Bedfords had lived in before going to Dickens, and Benjamin was part of the group that helped out there. In fact, he was the Sunday School Director of the Mission. He was there that fateful Sunday afternoon of December 7, 1941 when the Japanese attacked Pearl Harbor, plunging the U.S. into full participation in World War II.

Only one person from the sponsoring church actually spoke Spanish. This was a missionary named Edith Mims who interpreted for everyone. When a native Spanish-speaking preacher from Mexico became available, Edith resigned so that her salary could go to the pastor, and she moved to the little community of Pleasant Hill, one mile from the Texas border, where she taught school for a living. The small congregation of the Pleasant Hill Baptist Church had recently suffered a split and was without a pastor. Miss Mims suggested inviting some of the young men from the First Baptist Church of Clovis to fill the pulpit.

So it was that Leonard and Benjamin found themselves at Pleasant Hill one Sunday. Leonard preached in the morning and Benjamin that night. Benjamin was asked to preach again the next two Sundays. One of the deacons, a farmer named Gordon Smith, drove him back and forth between Clovis and Pleasant Hill. When Mr. Smith showed up at the meat market to talk to him on yet another Saturday about the next day, Benjamin came close to having a panic attack. This was beginning to look serious. What if the church actually asked him to be the pastor? It was impossible: he was only fifteen years old!

Work was especially heavy that day because the butcher was sick and Benjamin had to pick up the slack and clean the meat section. He told Mr. Smith he was going to have to stay late and that perhaps it would be better to find someone else to preach on Sunday. At five o'clock the farmer was back.

"Did you find anyone?" asked Benjamin.

"Didn't try to," answered Mr. Smith.

"The dairy man called in sick as well, so I'm going to have to stay and clean and close up."

"I'll wait."

Brother Gordon waited until Benjamin finished at eleven and took him to Pleasant Hill. The next morning the church held a business meeting and voted to call Benjamin Bedford as their next pastor. So Benjamin became a pastor at fifteen years of age and his friend Leonard was called soon afterwards to lead the congregation in St. Vrain. They were ordained together, and the ordination sermon was delivered by Dr. E.D. Head, President of Southwestern Baptist Seminary in Fort Worth, Texas, who happened to be in Clovis to preach at a revival.

Benjamin had no idea that Dr. Head was considered a notable scholar and one of the most outstanding men in the Baptist world at that time. He met him in the back seat of a car, on the way to Mrs. Lovett's funeral. She had been the matriarch of a prominent family with close ties to both FBC in Clovis and the church in Pleasant Hill. The pastors arranged to meet in Pleasant Hill, where Mr. Barbee would deliver the sermon and Benjamin would read the Scripture. Someone gave Benjamin and the personable visiting preacher a ride. On the road, Benjamin was thumbing through his Bible nervously when Dr. Head asked if he could help in any way.

"This is my first funeral," confided Benjamin. "I'd like to be sure I'm pronouncing everything correctly." The great man put his arm around Benjamin's shoulders and read through the passage with him to be sure he got all the words right.

The First Baptist Church of Clovis set aside eighty dollars in its budget for a scholarship to Eastern New Mexico College in nearby Portales. That year there were no college students, so the deacons voted to give the money to Benjamin to buy a car for an easier commute to Pleasant Hill. He found a Model B Ford for seventy-five dollars and that was the car he drove until he went to college.

Benjamin was soon stretched to the limit between school, work and church. He couldn't quit his job because he needed it to support his mother and himself. When the deacons became aware of the situation, they made him an offer: if he quit his job and devoted his Saturdays to visitation, the church would make up the difference. This arrangement continued until he finished high school. That summer he and his mother moved to the parsonage in Pleasant Hill, expecting Benjamin to spend his weekends there and attend school at Wayland Baptist College in between.

It had long been taken for granted that Benjamin would go to college. By the time he was in junior high school he knew that he was meant for full-time Christian service and, with the guidance of his pastor and other church leaders, he understood the need to prepare himself as well as possible, first in undergraduate school and later at the seminary. His entire family was in favor of him furthering his education but some, especially A.T., hoped he would get over this quixotic notion of being a pastor and go into something a bit more lucrative for all that effort, such as engineering or medicine.

He decided early on to go to Wayland and made several trips to Plainview to get the lay of the land. He was even offered the opportunity of starting a semester early, since by the middle of his senior year he lacked only one credit, Latin, to graduate. The college was willing to allow him to make it up later, but Benjamin finally chose not to rush things and to graduate with his classmates

Vignettes
1944-1964

A Bombshell

Gordon Smith turned onto Pile Street in downtown Clovis and brought the Chevy to a halt in front of the Central Baptist Church. Benjamin climbed out, stood up and shook out his trouser legs. The light breeze dried out his damp shirt and back by the time he reached the door of the church building.

"Pastor's expecting you," smiled the secretary as she ushered him into the office. Benjamin had first met Dr. Aulick during his senior year in high school. As President of the Student Council, one of his duties was to organize and preside over student assemblies. Visiting speakers included businessmen, pastors and a variety of professionals. Benjamin had met with Dr. Aulick to invite him and had learned some of his background.

Dr. Aulick was outstanding in many ways. He was definitely the most highly educated man Benjamin had ever met. He held an undergraduate degree from the University of New Mexico and several graduate degrees, including two doctorates, from Colgate University, Southwestern Baptist Seminary and the University of Delaware. He had been a pioneer in student work as the first traveling secretary of the Texas Baptist Student Missionary Movement, the forerunner of the Baptist Student Union, better known as the "BSU". He had pastored several well-known churches, including University Baptist Church in Austin, Texas and Trinity Baptist Church in Oklahoma City. He had taught at Oklahoma Baptist University for several years and was now pastor of the Central Baptist Church of Clovis during a leave of absence.

In spite of these impressive credentials, there was no denying that both Dr. Aulick and his wife were somewhat peculiar. They were dignified and proper, but at first glance they struck the observer as rather intense, stiff and artificial. This was probably simply due to the fact that he wore a toupee and that she dyed her hair jet black. Nevertheless, they were in fact down-to-earth, kind and warm-hearted people, always willing to give a helping hand. Now Dr. Aulick welcomed Benjamin, waved him into a chair and at last explained what the urgent summons was all about.

"Benjamin, I've been invited to fill the Bible Chair at Eastern New Mexico College and I've accepted. They are going all out and conditions are optimum. I thought of you immediately. I would really like for you to consider going to Eastern instead of Wayland."

It was a bombshell. Benjamin had everything neatly planned out but, since he genuinely respected Dr. Aulick's opinion and the great man had taken a special interest in him, he gave his advice careful consideration. Eastern New Mexico had originally been established as a teacher's college and opened its doors to its first one hundred sixty-five students in 1934. By 1940 it had become a four-year degree-granting college and was now hard at work on gaining university accreditation. Eastern had made tremendous efforts to hire excellent professors. Because of the war, enrollment was down, and this translated into small classes and close faculty-student relationships. Curricula and standards were very strict and demanding; as a result, the school offered a first-rate education. By 1949 Eastern officially became Eastern New Mexico University, well on its way to becoming the third largest university in the state.

Benjamin carefully weighed the pros and cons before coming to a decision. That is how he came to enroll in Eastern New Mexico College in Portales and never made it to Plainview or Wayland Baptist College.

Benjamin Meets His Match

Benjamin and Leonard strolled around downtown Portales and stopped at the Ben Franklin five-and-ten-cent store to pick up some supplies. Freshman Week had arrived at Eastern New Mexico College and Benjamin enrolled with a scholarship from the Baptist Convention of New Mexico that covered his registration and tuition fees.

"Oh, look!" exclaimed Leonard, spotting one of the clerks. "Come over here, Benjamin. I want you to meet La Nell. Hi, La Nell! This is my friend Benjamin Bedford. Benjamin, meet La Nell Watson."

As they shook hands, Benjamin thought, *"So this is La Nell Watson!"* He already knew some of her family. In fact, her brother John and sister-in-law Evelyn were members of his church. And her sister La Wanna was married to Herbert Bergstrom, pastor of nearby Ranchvale, so they met quite often at Associational gatherings. She was always extolling her sister's virtues and he had been leery of any matchmaking efforts. Although he was naturally very interested in girls, his tight schedules and finances had pretty much ruled out dating up to now.

Of course, he should have known that La Nell would be very good-looking if she resembled her sister at all. Here were the same long legs and elegant figure, the same fair skin set off by dark eyes and hair. But these big brown eyes sparkled with a light all of their own. Never had he seen a look that communicated so much liveliness, intelligence and love of life.

For her part, La Nell duly noted Benjamin and filed him away mentally as "Leonard's Friend" and "John's Pastor." Nevertheless, that night was the only time she ever mentioned meeting anyone in her diary: the entry for August 18, 1944 read "Met Benjamin Bedford."

When John Watson and Nora Land married, they had subscribed to the advanced notion of having only two children. They soon had two healthy sons, Kenneth and Maurice. When Maurice began growing out of the toddler stage, John sighed, "I miss the patter of little feet." So then came William Land (better known as "W.L." or "Dub"). But when W.L. was no longer a toddler, John began longing for another little one, and so on, until the family grew to include John Lewis, La Wanna, La Nell and Thomas. Instead of limiting their child-bearing years to their twenties as they had originally planned, the couple extended them well into their forties.

After four boys, La Wanna was definitely Sister with a capital "S" and reverently placed on a pedestal. But La Nell was everyone's pet and plaything. Her father and brothers rough-housed with her and let her tag along everywhere. In return, they were the only ones ever allowed to call her by the nickname "Nell." She was quite the tomboy and loved sports and horseback riding. She regularly traded indoor chores with her sister, as she much preferred milking cows and working in the fields to being stuck tamely indoors.

John was a vital, hard-working, fun-loving, charismatic character. He came from central Texas and loved "Big D" so much that he named his second son after it: Dallas Maurice. It was in Rogers, near Temple and Waco, where he had met Nora at the single church building that served Baptist and Methodist preachers on alternating Sundays. He sat behind her and fell in love with the perfect curve of her neck beneath an elegant bun and hat. He wouldn't hear of her cutting her beautiful hair for over two decades. He was always brimming with enthusiasm and plans, while she was the steady one, but she could seldom resist when he really turned on the charm.

One such occasion was when he wanted to buy a Whippet, the smart, speedy car that had taken the nation by storm in the late 1920s. He was all for it but Nora was skeptical. As they stood looking at it, John swung three-year-old La Nell high in the air, passed her through the window and sat her inside the steering wheel, a button in the middle of which acted as starter, headlight and horn control all in one, asking, "Do you like it, honey?" John and La Nell together were too much to resist.

John was the complete extrovert, friendly and interested in all sorts of people, machines and games. He got to know the Hispanic farm hands and fell in love with their language. Much to Nora's chagrin, he often spent long evening hours listening to Mexican radio stations and picked up quite a smattering of Spanish.

When La Wanna started school she felt a burning desire to teach: "When I grow up, I'm going to get a divorce and teach school!" She couldn't wait until she had the longed-for degree, so she began practicing on her little sister, who was four years younger. She would force La Nell to sit still while she rehashed the day's lessons and, if she started to squirm or tried to leave, La Wanna would smack her on the head with a large comb she kept handy for the purpose. In spite of this stern approach, she must have been a good teacher, because when La Nell finally started school, late because of having to work in the fields, she was so far advanced that she went through the first three grades in one year.

La Nell was amazed at the answers some of her classmates gave on the first day of school when the teacher was attempting to collect information for the school records:

"What's your name, sonny?"

"Johnny."

"Johnny what?"

"Just Johnny."

"How old are you?"

A shrug.

"What's your daddy's name?"

"Daddy."

And so on.

La Nell spent her first years on a farm near Lorenzo, a rural community eighteen miles east of Lubbock, Texas. Her first friend and playmate outside the family was the neighbors' little deaf-mute son. Before he was sent to the Deaf School in Austin, where he learned to speak and lip-read, the children developed their own code and communicated perfectly. He would come over on his fat little pony Molly and they would take turns riding Sometimes they would play tag and explore beneath the house, which was set up off the ground, or stack the wooden blocks that were left over when it was built. Before going home, he went through the unvarying ritual of counting everything in his pockets to make sure he took back every item he had brought with him.

He was not the only interesting neighbor. One family had a regular procession of children. There was always a baby draped like a towel over an older sibling's arm and it was fascinating to watch them race around in their games or chores with the head of the current year's infant bobbing up and down. Amazingly, none of the babies ever came to grief but grew into extremely sturdy children.

One day five-year-old La Nell was sent to play at a neighbor's house. She had a grand time and was eating popcorn when she was informed that she had a brand-new baby brother, Thomas, a totally unexpected piece of news. She was not the only one in the dark about the time of his arrival. The family often recalled the trip to Grandmother Land's funeral. There were so many of them packed into the car that the luggage was placed on the running board. Unfortunately, another vehicle sideswiped them and, although no one was injured, their bags flew in every direction and their clothes were strewn all over the highway. Tom wanted to know where he was when all of this happened.

"You weren't there, Tom. It was before your time."

"No, I was there. You just couldn't see me 'ccs I was riding on the fender!"

When his wife passed away, Grandfather Land turned over his two properties in Rogers to Nora and Bertha, and divided his time between his two daughters' homes, although he lived mainly with Nora and her family. Like most farmers, the Watsons were hard hit by the droughts and the Depression, and when they decided to move to Cone, in Crosby County, about thirty-five miles northeast of Lubbock, Grandfather Land went with them. C.C. (Christopher Columbus) Land was the shortest adult in the family at around five feet, seven inches; even his wife had been taller than he. La Nell adored him and felt that he was everything a grandfather should be: he had twinkly blue eyes and a ready laugh, and he was never too busy to hold her on her lap and give her the benefit of his considerable story-telling talents. There was only one thing she would have changed about him: used to her clean-shaven father and brothers, she disliked the tickling of his long, silky beard. Grandfather Land was devoted to La Nell and spent many hours helping to nurse her through a serious bout of pneumonia. Later on he contracted pneumonia himself and died. La Nell was devastated and could never rid herself of the nagging fear that he had caught it from her.

When her father died, Nora was forced to sell the property in Rogers to meet the medical and funeral expenses. To supplement their income from farming, they opened up a sideline renovating mattresses and set up the equipment in the barn. That was also where the men played dominoes and smoked. When the competition got too rowdy, Nora would gather up a handful of tiles and fling them into the potbellied stove, effectively suspending the game until they could afford a new set.

The family decided on yet another move, this time to Roosevelt County in the High Plains of New Mexico. Under Spanish rule in the 17th century, this area became known as the Llano Estacado, in English "staked plain," most likely a description of the arresting yucca plants with which the flat terrain was abundantly impaled. Comanche Indians dominated the region during the early 19th century and used it as their hunting grounds, subsisting mainly off of buffalo, but the last of the Native Americans were captured in 1874 and taken to a reservation in Oklahoma, paving the way for cattlemen to set up ranches in the area. A well-known watering hole was Portales Springs. It flowed out of a series of cave openings in a caliche cliff and fed a small lake. The rocky ledge from which it emerged resembled a Spanish porch, for which it was named. In 1898 newly laid tracks carried the first passenger train through the area. Portales was founded as a cattle-shipping point on the railroad and many towns sprang up on the High Plains alongside the tracks. Later others were founded by merchants to serve the ranchers and homesteaders who followed.

Roosevelt County was named after the twenty-sixth president of the United States, Theodore Roosevelt, and Portales became the county seat. Some of the secondary communities were Elida, Floyd, Dora, Causey, Arch, Kenna, Lingo, Milnesand, Pep and Rogers. Settlers had two main reasons for moving to Roosevelt County: one was the railroad and the other was the availability of shallow water. Homesteaders could take their picks and shovels, dig fifteen-foot wells and have plenty of water for domestic use, while most of the settlers outside of the Portales Valley had to haul drinking water from a few wells set up by ranchers until they could afford to drill wells of their own.

La Nell was to go to grade school, junior high, high school and college in Roosevelt County. At first the Watsons lived on a ranch near Elida, twenty-five miles southwest of Portales. The older brothers would ride out into the countryside looking for free-ranging mustangs. They rounded them up, tamed them and sold them. Of course they kept some of them for riding and working, including a beautiful mare they called "Nell" and gave to their little sister. One day in 1934 John Lewis came home with startling news. He had been out riding when he came across a parked car. He recognized the couple sleeping in it from pictures in the paper and the car from the description on the radio: it was the famous Texan gangsters Bonnie and Clyde, on the run in a stolen car after breaking jail to free one of their gang members and murdering two police officers. The manhunt ended soon afterwards in Louisiana, where the couple was shot to death by the police.

This was by far the most difficult time for the family, and not just because of the dire financial situation. John contracted pneumonia in 1935. He was hospitalized in Portales, but antibiotics were not yet available and, exhausted by hard work, his lungs weakened by years of heavy smoking, he was gone in a few days. Nora was shattered and appeared to have buried the will to live along with her husband's body. She withdrew into herself and became listless and depressed. The family doctor decided to use shock tactics:

"Miz Watson, if you go on like this, you are going to die. And then what will happen to these children? You have to pull yourself together!"

Nora did pull herself together. She moved the family to a nearby "truck farm" in Bethel, some ten miles west of Portales. There they grew all sorts of vegetables: okra, potatoes, beans, tomatoes, corn and peanuts, besides picking crops for others and hauling goods. Up to now all of the children had still been living at home, except for Kenneth, who had married and was farming in

West Texas. One by one the older sons began to marry and move out. When only La Wanna, La Nell and Tom were left, the little family moved to a smaller house in Bethel, and Nora cooked for the school district's cafeterias. They also lived in Mesa for a short time, where they had a wind powered charger that provided them with their first home electricity.

La Nell had long bus rides every day, first to the elementary school in Elida and later to the high school in Floyd. They were small and limited in what they offered. Nevertheless, La Nell loved school and picked up every scrap of knowledge available. She became a voracious reader and checked a new book out of the library every day. At night she would crawl into bed with the book. Before long her mother would call out:

"La Nell, put down that book, turn out the light and go to sleep."

"Just one more chapter!"

In a little while her mother would call out again: "La Nell, I told you to turn that thing off and go to sleep! It's late."

"Just one more page!"

She took every class the high school offered. In addition to the academic subjects, she studied typing, shorthand and bookkeeping. She even took Home Economics and, while the teacher showed the other students how to sew a straight seam (which she had learned to do on paper when she was so small that she had had to stand to reach the needle while she pedaled the machine with one foot), she made three outfits, including a suit. She was on the school volleyball and softball teams, and won the intramural competitions with them every year.

La Nell was quite popular, and there were always boys willing to drive all the way out to her house and take her to movies or parties, usually in Portales, although she made it very clear that she just wanted to have fun and was not ready or willing to settle down because she was going to college. She had the best grades of her class, but during her senior year she had an appendectomy that forced her to miss school for several weeks. On the pretext of some technicality over her absences, another student with better connections was named valedictorian in her stead, a position that went with a scholarship to Eastern New Mexico College. Her math teacher, Mr. Tolliver, was so incensed at this underhanded maneuver that he fought tooth and nail for her until she was awarded the scholarship she needed in order to enroll.

In spite of having been such a pet of her father's and of having spent so much time out of doors, La Nell had a special bond with her mother. When John died, it was not to the moody teenage La Wanna that she turned, but to ten-year-old La Nell, who was to become her lifelong confidante. But there was another reason for Nora feeling something special for her second daughter. When La Nell was three years old, she contracted diphtheria and hovered between life and death for days. Nora sent up anguished prayers for her little girl's life to be spared. Not once, but several times, she sensed a strange answer: "*Give her to me. Are you willing to let her serve me far away?*" Nora agreed. She did not tell her daughter about it until she was grown and had already chosen her path in life but rather treasured up all these things and pondered them in her heart.

Meanwhile, she set about ensuring that La Nell would be prepared for whatever the future held in store for her, and it was understood as a matter of course that she was meant to go to college. Although she was not indulgent, Nora devoted time to her daughter, talking to her and encouraging her. She never sent her off to school without an approving, "You look very nice today!"

Nora set high standards in everything she did. She was somewhat of a domestic genius. To begin with, she was a natural chef: she knew when a concoction was right by its look, feel and smell. Sometimes, when she tried something totally new, she prepared an advance "tester," a small sample that she would cook to find out if it needed tweaking. When she was asked for recipes, the directions were baffling: a little of this, a handful of that, a pinch of this, a dash of that. Like most women of the time, she did the sewing for her family, but she was more than just a seamstress: she was a designer. She didn't need patterns to turn out clothes that fit perfectly and were in line with the latest fashions. She had cousins who lived in Washington, D.C. and moved in the rarified circles of the nation's Congress. When they sent her boxes of the very expensive clothes they no longer wished to wear, she would pick them apart and use the beautiful material to make dresses. Sometimes she even felt guilty that they had such high quality clothes when the neighbors had to make do with flour sacks.

Church was a key aspect of their lives. They attended rural churches that were so small they could not afford to pay a pastor's salary but, since they were near Portales, the pulpit was often filled by the current Bible professor from Eastern New Mexico College. Nora was a devoted Sunday School teacher who taught her class on Sunday morning and began preparing for the next lesson that same evening. On ironing day she would prop her Bible and Sunday School material on the table in front of her so she could study while she worked.

La Nell remembered being eight years old and looking around the congregation during the sermon, thinking who should be making this or that decision in response to the message, until the day she realized that she herself had never made one. She was later baptized in Elida by a pastor named Kirkendall. Even so, she often felt uncomfortable during the services and wondered what could be wrong. When she finally got up the nerve to ask about it, her Sunday School teacher suggested that she might be feeling a call to some kind of service. After that, she knew that someday she would do something special and determined to be prepared when the time came.

So, throughout her school years La Nell heard top-notch scholars hold forth, such as Dr. Barrett and Dr. Humphreys. She also got to know them personally over the delicious Sunday lunches to which her mother often invited them. And they got to know her and take a personal interest in her progress. La Nell participated in everything, from helping at the church office to coordinating the children's activities as Superintendent of Vacation Bible School during her high school years.

When it was time for La Nell to go to college, Nora and Tom moved with her to Portales, where they attended the First Baptist Church (La Wanna had married soon after graduating from high school and now lived in nearby Ranchvale). Pastor Barnes and his wife Helen hospitably opened their home to the college students every Sunday night, and there La Nell soon made new friends, the closest of which was Earlene. Nora worked as seamstress for the Children's Home and La Nell got a job as a clerk at the Ben Franklin Store. She plunged into college life and loved every minute of it.

Work and Play

Very little money, very little experience and a packed schedule did not deter Benjamin from getting to know La Nell better: the war had imposed austerity on everyone; he trusted his instincts; and he worked the plethora of activities to his advantage.

Austerity was nothing new for either Benjamin or La Nell, whose childhood had been shaped by the Great Depression and adolescence by World War II. Like everyone else, they listened avidly to the radio as President Franklin D. Roosevelt's famous "Fireside Chats" shifted from the economy to the war effort, and Edward Murrow brought live reports directly from London. Posters plastered throughout town exhorted the population to make special efforts: a woman in a factory uniform flexing sturdy arm muscles was depicted below the words "We Can Do It"; a man in overalls thrust his shovel into the soil as an incentive to "Grow More Food. Dig for Victory!"; a smiling soldier drank out of a metal cup between captions that urged civilians to "Do with less–so they'll have enough!" and promised that "Rationing gives you your fair share."

The Food Rationing Program was launched in the spring of 1942 to avoid public anger with shortages and to prevent the wealthy from buying up all of the available supplies. A system of coupons, stamps and points was soon perfected, and covered just about everything: food, clothing, fuel and all types of equipment. People usually registered for their coupons at the local schools— one member of the family was sent and asked to describe the rest of the household since distribution depended on family size. Coupon books allowed their holders to buy specific amounts of some goods but were not a guarantee of availability. There were four types of rationing. Uniform coupon rationing provided equal shares for all consumers, for example, for sugar. Point rationing provided equivalent shares for all of the items in a given group, such as processed foods, meats, fat and cheese. Differentiated coupon rationing depended on need, for things like gasoline and fuel oil. Finally, certificate rationing distributed industrial products by application based on need, for example, tires, cars, stoves and typewriters. In addition, coupons were stamped red or blue: "red stamp" rationing covered all meats, butter, fats, oil and cheese, for which a weekly number of points were awarded, with expiration dates; "blue stamp" rationing concerned canned, bottled and frozen fruits and vegetables, juices, dry beans and processed foods, such as soups, baby food and ketchup. Ration stamps became a kind of currency and, inevitably, a black market sprang up to get around the restrictions. There were also recycling drives for aluminum cans, all sorts of metals, paper and rubber. By 1945 there were twenty million of the so-called "Victory Gardens" in which families grew up to forty percent of all of the vegetables in the United States.

Although some people resorted to coupon trading and the black market to satisfy their needs, there were many good neighbors who shared what they had. When Benjamin's high school class was preparing for the junior-senior banquet, they found they were short on sugar for the punch. Resourceful Mrs. Bayliss, their Latin teacher and faculty sponsor, drove out to Pleasant Hill to pick up sugar donated by Lola Glover, a member of Benjamin's congregation. As pastor, he had a slightly larger allotment of gasoline than the average civilian, but even so it was often not enough for all of his driving, and the farmers, who had a bigger share of fuel, would fill up his tank from time to time. La Nell and her family, on the other hand, did not own a car and, since Portales was a small town, went everywhere on foot.

Besides school, Benjamin and La Nell were involved in a wide variety of organizations and activities. One of the most important was the Baptist Student Union, affectionately known as the BSU, which had enthusiastic faculty support and the sponsorship of Dr. Aulick, one of its national pioneers. The BSU offered an instant safe and familiar social environment, especially for Baptist students near and far from home, and warmly welcomed all others. Each local BSU elected its own officers among the students on campus and sent delegates to state and national associations to coordinate joint efforts. In addition to spiritual support, including daily noontime devotionals and prayer time, the BSU organized parties and social events where students could get together and have a good time safely and without having to spend money.

La Nell was already a sophomore and one of the BSU leaders. That year she was sent to the State Convention in Las Cruces, where she was elected State Secretary. Benjamin had planned to take an active part in the BSU, but got more than he had bargained for when the local President-elect did not attend after all, and Benjamin was chosen to replace him. This meant that both he and La Nell were involved in organizing all of the year's activities.

The first social event offered by the BSU to welcome the students to the new school year was a "Sadie Hawkins" party, a phenomenon that had swept across the nation's college campuses, inspired by the "Lil' Abner" comic strip. La Nell and Benjamin not only helped organize the party and the invitations, but were also on the clean-up crew. When Benjamin saw La Nell in the short, ragged-edged black skirt of her Daisy Mae costume that night, he quickly decided that cleaning up would be no chore.

The BSU's reputation in the community was so high that it was invited to participate in a radio program which featured local organizations on a rotating basis. Benjamin was the natural choice for announcer because of his beautiful, resonant bass voice, which had caused him to have broadcasting urged upon him as a career as soon as his voice changed in junior high. La Nell had a part in their very first program, and Benjamin got so flustered by her nearness across the two-sided microphone that he couldn't even think of her name, and had to resort to a formal presentation as "Miss Watson."

The school basketball and football teams offered weekly games, and most of the students turned out to watch them. Benjamin realized that they were a golden opportunity. He worked up his nerve all week and finally asked, "Are you going to the basketball game?"

"Oh, yes," answered La Nell. "I always go with the Glee Club."

All through the first half of the game he could see her from the other side of the court, following the game intently, laughing and cheering with her friends. At half-time he went over to say hello and was glad he did, because it turned out that she was through with her Glee Club obligations for the day and was free for the rest of the event. So they watched the second half together and that night he walked her home for the very first time.

But they were not just spectators: both La Nell and Benjamin played intramural sports. La Nell played volleyball and softball for Pi Epsilon, the honorary Business School society, while Benjamin, who belonged to the Ministerial Alliance, was on its softball and volleyball teams. Both of them pitched, in the hard, fast, no-nonsense underhand style then in vogue. Benjamin fell into the habit of watching the women's games in the late afternoon, thereby increasing his opportunities to walk La Nell home.

He even took up tennis when he discovered that La Nell loved that sport. The tennis court was next to the Administration Building and had a very important feature from Benjamin's point of view: a water fountain. Not only was it refreshing after a lively game, but it brought the drinkers' heads very close together. At times they played alone and at others they played doubles with Leonard and Earlene. On one of these occasions, filled with competitive spirit, Benjamin called out, "Serve a double, La Nell!"

"What?" gasped a winded Leonard. "I can't hit one at a time, let alone two!"

Of course they were at college mainly to study, and study they did, because the school had very strict standards. Students were required to have an average of at least ninety-six out of one hundred points in order to earn an "A". Benjamin and La Nell were in different years and programs. It was Benjamin's first year and his major had the fascinating name of Metaphysical Sciences, a broad liberal arts degree that offered firm grounding in history, philosophy, religion and sociology, among other subjects. La Nell, on the other hand, was already a sophomore, and was studying toward a Business Education degree. As a result, they only had one class together: Speech, taught by P.M. Bailey. This professor always alternated the order in which he called on students to present, starting either at the beginning or at the end of the alphabet, so that it was always either Benjamin ("B" for Bedford) or La Nell ("W" for Watson) who started things off.

Benjamin missed several days of class when his brother L.D. became very ill and had to be hospitalized in Odessa. Worried, Billie and Tennie asked Benjamin to take them there. He was able to do so because he had traded in his rickety Model B for a nice little blue

Ford coupe that could seat up to six people at a pinch. When they returned, he needed to catch up on the school work he had missed. Although the men's dormitory was quite close to his home, he chose to walk across campus to La Nell's house to get the Speech assignment.

She lived with her mother and brother in a small three-room dwelling: kitchen, living room and one bedroom with two double beds–one for Nora and La Nell, and one for Tom. La Nell herself opened the door and welcomed him in. She had on an apron and the delicious aroma of French toast enveloped her. La Nell looked up the assignment and introduced Benjamin to her mother. When the door shut after him, Nora told her daughter, "That boy is in love with you–he just doesn't know it yet."

La Nell no longer worked at the Ben Franklin store. She had been approached by the college upon the recommendation of the Business professors to take the position of Assistant Registrar. The Registrar's Office was the administrative heart of the college and affected not only the careers of the students from the time they applied for admission to graduation but the way the faculty did its job as well. There were four main duties: academic recordkeeping, room scheduling, statistical reporting and campus information.

The Registrar was in charge of overseeing the application process, verifying information against requirements, maintaining records of student grades, compiling the list of students eligible for graduation, issuing official transcripts, arranging class and event schedules and locations, gathering statistical data for the College and for governmental authorities and providing information on the college's academic requirements, course offerings and registration procedures. Eastern New Mexico's Registrar had been planning to take a leave of absence to work on her Master's Degree. As a result, La Nell became Acting Registrar and, although Dean Gossard's name appeared on the official documents, it was she who kept the administrative wheels of the college turning.

A group of friends began gathering when she got off work: Benjamin, Leonard Lane and his current girlfriend (first Earlene and then Daisy), and Jimmy Curry and his Isabelle. Jimmy had a short arm, paralyzed by polio, but that didn't keep him from working for the College in maintenance. His tasks included keeping the Coke machines stocked. After they paid for the drinks, he would open up the machine and get the ice-cold slushy ones from the back. Then they would flop into seats in an empty room and catch up on their day.

Benjamin was gone to Pleasant Hill most of the weekend fulfilling his duties as pastor. He soon found out about the Fellowship Hour La Nell's church offered to college students on Sunday night at the Barnes' home and, if he worked things just right, he could usually be back in time to go. After two packed days of visiting church members and preaching twice on Sunday, Benjamin would take his mother home. Worried about his long hours, she would tell him, "You ought to go to bed and rest." He seldom took this advice, but rather hurried off to the Barnes' house for some light-hearted conversation and the chance to see La Nell safely home.

It was some time before La Nell discovered Benjamin's age. She had never thought about it. He was tall and well developed, with broad shoulders and strong hands, and he had been a pastor for at least a couple of years: clearly he was a grown man. When she found out that he was actually seventeen, two full years her junior, she was appalled. He was just a baby! She would simply have to find a way to discourage his increasingly apparent intentions. But every time she worked up the nerve to break it off, he would do something particularly charming, such as bring her flowers, and she would put if off once more.

Demobbed

"I'm worried about La Nell," confided Dr. Aulick. "Is she going blind?"

Benjamin looked confused.

"It's just that I see you leading her around everywhere by the hand," chuckled the professor slyly.

La Nell and Benjamin had become an item. They often double-dated with Leonard and his now definitive girlfriend Daisy. La Nell and Leonard's birthdays were one day apart in January, and they began a tradition of celebrating them with a combined party. Benjamin and Leonard often preached at youth revivals together and planned outings with the girls when they got back. One day they had arranged to meet them at 8:00 but had a flat tire on the way back from Texico. By the time they had stopped at home to wash and change they were late for their date. Benjamin apologized and described the messy night-time tire-changing operation.

"What did Leonard do?" the girls wanted to know.

"He held the flashlight."

It wasn't easy to get any time alone. Benjamin frequently visited La Nell at home but, although her mother was discreet, her little brother, who until recently had shunned the company of his mother and sister in public to the extent of walking on the other side of the street, showed an inopportune partiality for Benjamin's company. Besides being naturally curious and eager to annoy his sister, Tom had grown up without a father and, since his older brothers had left home long ago, he was starved for male companionship and role models. He was always hanging around. Benjamin played catch with him in the yard and even pitched for the softball team Tom organized to play in the City League with his co-workers from the Ben Franklin store where he now held a part-time job.

However, one morning Benjamin had La Nell all to himself. They were playing with a Ouija board and laughing at the silly answers. Their heads came close together and Benjamin seized the opportunity to steal a kiss.

"Do you think that was wrong?" he asked rather breathlessly.

"It depends on what you mean by it," she replied.

That opened up the way for increasingly frank and serious conversations about their feelings for each other and their future together. Often these talks took place outside, away from curious ears. During one of these, Benjamin suddenly said:

"Suppose that I felt called to missions."

"Why? Do you feel that way?"

"Not necessarily, but what if I did?"

"Then I'd be willing," replied La Nell. Later she laughed that, as usual, he had made sure that he had every angle covered.

On the ministerial front, Benjamin had received an invitation to pastor First Baptist Church of Portales' mission at Kennedy Heights. The congregation at Pleasant Hill was going strong and Benjamin felt that it was the right time for a change. A nice garage apartment became available for Benjamin and his mother, with a little more room for their combined belongings from the parsonage they had been occupying on the weekends in Pleasant Hill and the tiny house they lived in during the week in Portales. They soon settled in and Tennie resumed the now traditional meals she prepared for Benjamin's colleagues who commuted to regional congregations and returned to meager cupboards in their student lodgings.

The Kennedy Heights Mission met in a small white one-room building southeast of the college campus, between the school and the Baptist Children's Home. It was in one of the poorest sections of town and was home to a fascinating mixture of people, from the down-and-out to college students. There were very few material resources available but there was a lot of ingenuity. Up to four Bible classes met simultaneously, so they rigged up a system of overhead wires and curtains to partition the space as needed. During Benjamin's first year there were twenty-two baptisms. He preached, taught, visited, presided over marriages and funerals and, in short, packed ten years' worth of experience into one.

All the while Benjamin continued to be active in Associational work. While he was pastor of the Pleasant Hill congregation he had been the Vacation Bible School Superintendent for the Plains Baptist Association, which covered Curry County. He had gone to Albuquerque with the statewide VBS promoter and visited all the churches in a two-to three-hundred mile radius with La Wanna's husband Herbert and W.C. Wright, respectively the Association's Clerk and President, setting up fifty VBS sites in the process. Vacation Bible School usually lasted one to two weeks in the summer, offering Bible school for the children in the afternoon and youth revivals at night. Now that he was at Kennedy Heights, Benjamin belonged to the Portales Baptist Association and was named its Training Union Director.

One summer day Benjamin and La Nell were returning from an Associational meeting with Pastor Barnes and heard over the radio that the Japanese had surrendered, so they drove straight to the First Baptist Church building to ring the bells in celebration. On a personal level, the end of the war was a relief because it meant that Benjamin's brother Ira could come home. News had been sketchy during the three years he was gone. His mother received brief missives that served mainly to let them know he was still alive. Once they heard through a friend that Ira had been ill with malaria. The first they knew of his return was a knock on the screen door and Ira's voice asking, "Aren't you going to open up?"

Ira was the first veteran in the family since Grandfather Anthony's stint in the Civil War. Lorenzo Anthony fought on both sides during the Civil War, but he was neither a turncoat nor a double agent. Following his convictions, the young man joined the Union Army. He was called home to bury his wife and child and, on his way to rejoin his regiment, he was captured by the rebels and forced to fight for the Confederate Army. Eventually he managed to escape and make his way back to the Union forces. When the war was over, he married a half-Choctaw Indian and raised a new family.

Ira, who knew he would be called up, had enlisted in the army and taken a six-week course as a medic. He was sent first to North Africa, then to Sicily and finally to France, following General Patton's army. He did not have to kill anyone but he saw a tremendous amount of carnage. The main objective of the medics was to get the wounded away from the front line. This often involved climbing out of foxholes during shelling or into no-man's land to help the fallen. Once he reached the wounded soldier, the medic had to make a brief examination, evaluate the injury, apply a tourniquet if necessary, clean the wound as well as possible, sprinkle sulfur powder on it, bandage it, and drag or carry the patient out of harm's way, often under enemy fire or artillery shelling. The Germans usually respected the Red Cross armband, but there were no guarantees. Although his experiences dimmed his sparkle, they did not quench it entirely. Every time he talked to Benjamin on the telephone, Ira murmured, "Vinegar, vinegar!" and that childhood episode became Benjamin's favorite illustration when he preached on the power of guilt.

Tying the Knot

La Nell wondered if she had made a terrible mistake. She even toyed with the idea of breaking the charged silence and asking Benjamin to turn the car around and take her back to Portales. She had had no inkling that Benjamin might have a frightening temper until they went to the car after the wedding reception to head out on their honeymoon.

When they decided to get married, Ben asked both of their mothers for permission. His own mother had to sign a legal authorization because her son was still technically a minor. Benjamin ceremoniously asked Nora for La Nell's hand in marriage.

"Would you be willing to give away your daughter?"

"No," was his prospective mother-in-law's stunning reply. Before he could react she added, "But I will gladly take on another son!"

They set their sights on the summer of '46. That would give them plenty of time to make all the necessary arrangements and save up some money. The summer before, Benjamin did odd jobs for the college, from cutting the grass with a tractor-pulled mower to cleaning classrooms, for which the school paid a flat rate, based on the time calculated to clean each room. This was a good deal for Benjamin, who could do the work in half the time.

La Nell took a summer position as secretary of the First Baptist Church and kept the typewriter and mimeograph humming as she prepared letters and churned out stencils and copies of bulletins and all sorts of material. In the fall she got an unexpected proposal. The nationwide shortage of teachers had hit her own high school alma mater in Floyd. Mr. Tolliver, her former math teacher and scholarship champion, suggested hiring La Nell to fill in the gap during the spring semester.

Since she was well ahead with her studies and could certainly use the extra income, she accepted. She taught typing, shorthand, bookkeeping and, as a special favor to Mr. Tolliver who would otherwise have had to do it, English. Because she didn't have a car, she rented a tiny apartment in Floyd and Benjamin drove her back and forth on the weekends, making lightning visits in between whenever he could. But after being accustomed to seeing each other every day, this separation soon became intolerable, and they decided to move the wedding date up to Thursday, April 18, taking advantage of the long Easter weekend.

It wasn't too complicated. They would live in the apartment Benjamin was renting. The only large item that had to be moved in was La Nell's piano, but there was another important item that had to be moved out—Benjamin's mother. However, she raised no objections but made plans to stay with Billie temporarily in Clovis and, when Ira got a place with her nephew Howard in Vetsville to go to college on the GI Bill, she moved in and kept house for them.

La Wanna was thrilled and went around looking like the cat that ate the cream. The ceremony would take place at La Nell's church, First Baptist, and her brother-in-law Herbert would perform the ceremony. Her sister was to be maid of honor and Leonard best man. Leonard's own marriage was coming up soon as well, and Benjamin joked that he was the best man at both weddings. Daisy had been helping out at the Kennedy Heights Mission, and the people there prepared a wedding shower. A red wagon heaped with gifts was rolled in, bearing a sign that said "Daisy and Leonard." When everybody gathered round, a second sign was revealed that read "La Nell and Benjamin" for a surprise double-wedding shower. Daisy also played an important role at Benjamin and La Nell's wedding. She sat by La Nell's three-year-old nephew Jimmy, who later reminisced fondly, "Remember when Daisy and I got married?"

The church was filled with relatives and friends from school and church. The student body was so small that students and professors all knew each other well. They had recently shared an experience that had brought them even closer together. Benjamin had asked his friends to pray for his brother L.D., who had never made a public profession of faith. One week L.D. came alone to get some dental work done in Clovis. He decided to hear his youngest sibling preach while he was there. It happened that Benjamin had been invited to fill the pulpit at FBC that Sunday. It was a thrilling moment for all of them when L.D. walked down the aisle. "What a good thing that I wasn't called upon to pray," said Dr. Aulick. "I don't think I would have made it!" Once he had made up his mind, L.D. didn't waste any time. He wanted his brother to baptize him, so it was arranged for that very next Wednesday.

This afternoon they were ready to share another big moment. Benjamin had attended class that morning and La Nell had worked in Floyd. In order to make it on time, she had actually taught class with her hair in curlers, but at six o'clock she was ready to glide down the aisle, resplendent in an elegant gold suit and frothy white blouse. There was a small reception and going-away dinner, held at the home of Dr. Floyd Golden, President of Eastern New Mexico College and member of the First Baptist Church. Benjamin's car was stowed away in his garage, where it was sure to be safe from pranksters.

Nevertheless, a couple of ingenious souls had discovered the hiding place and painted the car with newlywed slogans. When Benjamin saw the car, all he said was, "I asked you not to do that," but everyone present felt a scorching heat-wave blast over them. Dr. Golden took off his jacket, rolled up his sleeves and helped Benjamin wash off the paint. Then Benjamin and La Nell drove off, all in absolute silence, which lasted until they were half-way to Elida.

Suddenly, a deer bounded across the road, missing the car by inches and shaking its occupants into speech. Benjamin was recovering and ready to talk things over with La Nell, proving that he was not a monster after all and that he almost always succeeded in controlling his temper.

They spent the honeymoon in Roswell, where they went to the movies together for the first time. Unlike La Nell, who had been often with friends, Benjamin had spent his teenage years in a church whose pastor had frowned upon movies as a bad influence. They also went sightseeing to the Bottomless Lakes in New Mexico's first state park, sixteen miles southeast of Roswell.

The lakes consist of a chain of eight sinkholes, formed when water dissolved salt and gypsum deposits to form underground caverns. The domes collapsed under their own weight and the resulting depressions filled with water. The unique geology and water chemistry created a habitat for unusual plants and animals. The lakes' greenish-blue color creates the illusion that they are bottomless, and the myth was given life by cowboys who failed to reach the bottom after tying their saddle ropes together. Actually, they vary from seventeen to nineteen feet in depth. The deepest is crystal-clear, spring-fed Lea Lake.

La Nell and Benjamin attended the First Baptist Church of Roswell on Sunday morning and returned to Portales that afternoon. They stopped by Nora's house to pick up a set of dishes they had been given and went to church at Ranchvale that night. La Nell had arranged for a substitute to teach her classes the next week, so they got up at a leisurely hour and La Nell made hot biscuits. Just as she was sliding the pan out of the oven, there was a knock on the door: Herbert, La Wanna and Jimmie couldn't wait any longer, so they shared Benjamin and La Nell's very first breakfast at home as a married couple.

Monkey Business

"Dim it, brother, dim it!" exclaimed an exasperated Dr. Aulick, blinded by yet another set of high beams.

"It's a good thing we know you so well, or we might have understood something entirely different," teased La Nell.

They were on the way to the Plains Student Conference in Canyon, Texas. Now that they were married, Benjamin and La Nell were able to go almost everywhere together, and it was certainly a lot more fun that way. This particular conference closed with a social hour, and La Nell did her part by dedicating an anonymous poem on evolution that was making the rounds of the college campuses to Dr. Aulick:

> Three monkeys sat in a coconut tree
> Discussing things as they are said to be.
> Said one to the others, "Now listen, you two,
> There's a rumor around that can't be true,
>
> That man descended from our noble race.
> The very idea is a great disgrace.
> "No monkey has ever deserted his wife
> Starved her babies and ruined her life.
>
> And you've never known a mother monk
> To leave her babies with others to bunk
> Or pass from one to another
> Till they scarcely know who is their mother.
>
> "And another thing you'll never see,
> A monk build a fence round a coconut tree,
> And let the coconuts go to waste,
> Forbidding all other monks to taste;

Why, if I put a fence around a tree,
Starvation will force you to steal from me!
"Here's another thing that a monkey won't do:
Go out at night and get on a stew.

Or use a gun or club or knife
To take some other monkey's life.
Yes, man descended, the ornery cuss
But, brother, he didn't descend from us."

La Nell also knew quite a few of the popular morbid "Little Willie" *Ruthless Rhymes* and trotted them out with perfect timing to crack everyone up:

Little Willie in bows and sashes
Fell in the fire and was burned to ashes.
Though Winter's come and days grow chilly,
No one wants to poke up Willie.

Willie in his roguish way
Tipped Grandpa on the fire one day
Mother said, "My dear, that's cruel!
But of course it does save fuel."

Little Willie, pleasure bent,
Entombed his father in cement.
Mother said, "You little cad,
I think you're rather hard on Dad."

Almost every outing, however weighty and worthy, had its lighter side, like the time they piled into the car with five of their friends to support a colleague as he led the singing at a revival meeting. The pastor recognized the college group but evidently did not have too firm a grasp on their names as he announced, "And now Brother Buford Benrod will lead us in prayer." Benjamin was hard put to maintain the requisite pastoral solemnity with the pew rocking from the suppressed laughter of his six companions.

At times things could get positively bizarre. A sizable group from their church crammed into three or four cars for the ride to the State Training Union Convention in Ruidoso. On the way back they stopped for a sandwich. The place had several slot machines to tempt the tourists and almost everyone had a go to see what it was like, with no success. "Come on, Preacher! Give it a try!" Hoping to get them off his back and move on to something else, Benjamin stuck in a dime, pulled on the lever and was promptly showered by a large stream of coins, about twenty or thirty dollars' worth of them. After that, they called him "Jackpot Bedford."

As President of the New Mexico State BSU, Benjamin made his first trip outside of the New Mexico-Texas-Oklahoma area without La Nell, when he went all the way to the Ridgecrest Baptist Encampment near Ashville, North Carolina for the National Convention. Meanwhile, La Nell made a trip of her own to take Henry, a bright five-year-old from the Kennedy Heights Mission who had won the Associational Bible story-telling contest, to compete in the State championship.

It took a while for Benjamin and La Nell to settle into anything resembling a routine. La Nell commuted to Floyd until the end of the school year. Even though she wasn't officially a college student that semester, Dr. Bailey relayed requests for assistance with college radio productions through Benjamin. After a couple of months, a duplex became available on Pine Street and they took it, unaware that they had embarked on a lifelong pattern of frequent housing changes.

Meanwhile, Herbert and La Wanna made plans to go to Louisville, Kentucky to attend the Seminary but, before they went, Jimmy paid a visit to his aunt and uncle, entertaining them with his lively chatter on every subject. The bedtime Bible story involved a death and Jimmy explained: "Aunt La Nell, you're dead if your heart's not beating."

The next morning he was socializing with some construction workers when one of them asked him, "Are you married, sonny?"

Unwilling to disappoint the man completely, Jimmy replied, "No, but my daddy is!"

The Bergstroms' departure left the congregation at Ranchvale without a pastor, and the church lost no time in inviting Benjamin, who accepted and agreed to begin his service in the summer. He and La Nell had a choice to make: whether to live in Portales and commute to the church activities in Ranchvale or live at the parsonage and commute to school. At first they tried staying in Portales, but it soon proved to be too complicated, so they moved to the church's two-bedroom parsonage.

Although they were the first married couple inducted together into the Silver Key honor society, later to become Phi Beta Kappa, and Benjamin was named to the prestigious Cacique service organization and appeared in the "Who's Who in Colleges and Universities," they participated less and less in college activities as the pastorate increasingly absorbed their time. They arranged to take classes on Mondays, Wednesdays and Fridays so they wouldn't have to drive to Portales every day. The thirty-mile drive took quite a while because the road was in the process of being converted into a double highway, often forcing them to drive in a ditch. They usually stopped in Clovis to pick up their colleague Vernon Meeks at the Spanish Mission that held so many memories for Benjamin, and gave him a ride to the College in Portales.

The church at Ranchvale afforded a wide variety of challenges and opportunities. Visitation meant a lot of driving, since the members were spread over some sixty to seventy miles, beginning just outside of Clovis and going half-way to Melrose. The congregation was a good size, and Sunday School attendance was at about one hundred seventy-five. There was plenty of support from the backbone of the church: a dependable group of energetic and dedicated young married couples with small children and middle-aged couples with teenagers. La Nell and Benjamin opened up a fellowship hour modeled after the one they had attended at the Barnes' home in Portales, and built up a group of around twenty to thirty young people, mostly high-school students. La Nell taught junior children in Sunday School and young people in Training Union, besides organizing Vacation Bible School for around one hundred children in the summer. Apart from the more spiritual aspects, La Nell also trained the young ones for associational and state competitions in Bible-story telling, Bible sword drills and speech. She herself made it all the way to the State speech finals. For his part, in addition to the usual pastoral duties of preaching, visiting, counseling and organizing, Benjamin was named Clerk of the Plains Association. And in material terms, they had never been so well off. Although the salary was not much, it covered their expenses, they lived in a very comfortable house, and the church members kept them stocked with every kind of delicious food fresh from the farm.

Now that the war was over, the barracks in Ft. Sumner were dismantled and sold for construction material. While Eastern New

Mexico College took advantage of this opportunity to build a gymnasium and housing for married veterans, the congregation at Ranchvale bought enough to build a U-shaped addition to the church building and a garage for the parsonage. This, along with the church basement, was Benjamin and La Nell's first building project.

Not everything was smooth sailing, however. La Nell began to suffer from worrisome fainting spells that didn't seem to be wholly accounted for by the breakneck pace that stole away her appetite and only allowed for four to five hours of sleep at night. She began fainting every time she was startled, for example, when she didn't hear someone approach her, or when she got too excited at a sports event.

Very concerned, Benjamin took her to the doctor in Clovis. A rare heart arrhythmia was discovered and they were advised that pregnancy and delivery would be very dangerous for La Nell's health. This was crushing news because they both longed to have a family. They soon had the opportunity of caring for a two-year old child who had been entrusted to the Baptist Children's Home. He was a delightful little boy and they fell in love with him immediately. They would have liked nothing better than to adopt him, but his parents wanted him back; they only needed someone to give him temporary foster care.

Benjamin and La Nell took advantage of a Seminary reconnaissance visit in Fort Worth, Texas to make an appointment with a heart specialist in Amarillo on the way home. The doctor had startling but very welcome news: there was nothing at all wrong with La Nell's heart. It was simply in an unusual position—in the center and vertical rather than inclined to the left, and this was what caused the unusual rhythm. All she needed was iron for her anemia and some rest to be as good as new. There were no barriers to having children after all, but they never forgot the little boy they loved first.

The Graduates

"You are speaking at the pulpit. There is a couple at the back holding hands, their minds obviously far away. How do you get their attention?" asked Dr. Bailey during Benjamin's final oral examination at Eastern New Mexico College.

The trouble, thought Benjamin, was that it was extremely difficult to predict how people would react. There had been that junior boy, about nine or ten years old, during his first pastorate at Pleasant Hill, who had paid flatteringly close attention to a sermon based on an Old Testament text. His father later confided that at lunch his son had asked, "Daddy, what was that that Brother Benjamin said about his shack and a bed to go with it?" The message had been about Daniel's three friends in the fiery furnace: Shadrach, Meshach and Abednego.

Perceived shortcomings in the speaker's delivery were often unexpected, as in the case of the man from the Ranchvale congregation who told him, "Preacher, the only thing I don't like about your sermons is that they're too short—you finish so quick that I don't have time to go to sleep!" That same man's small son focused on other aspects of the speaker. One Sunday morning, when Benjamin made his way to the spot near the door where he always greeted the people as they left, he found his place taken by the little boy, who stuck out his hand in a perfect imitation of the pastor's manner and announced with great aplomb, "I'm the preacher today! How do you do?"

In spite of these considerations, Dr. Bailey's question was one of the easy ones. The oral exam that all candidates for graduation had to undergo was quite a harrowing experience. It was presided by the major professor but all of the faculty could attend and ask any question on any subject in order to determine whether or not the students were worthy of the degree they sought. La Nell had been through it the year before and, among other things, had been asked by an economics professor how to prevent an economic depression.

Benjamin and La Nell's time at Ranchvale had been truly delightful. The people were wonderful, and the young couple had both taught and learned a great deal. La Nell would have been happy to find a job teaching school and settle down to raise a family there. Benjamin also loved Ranchvale, but he was afraid that if he didn't go straight on to the Seminary he would get sidetracked and never complete his training.

They seriously considered going to Golden Gate Seminary in California, where Dr. Aulick would begin to teach the next fall and where they would have Leonard Lane as a classmate. Benjamin's mentor was once again instrumental in his choice of school. He recommended that they go to Southwestern Baptist Seminary in Fort Worth, Texas instead, which at this point in time had much more to offer. Golden Gate was a new school; it had been founded only four years before in Oakland at the Golden Gate Baptist Church, moving shortly thereafter to Berkeley. While it was in the process of establishing itself, Southwestern was a mature institution. It had grown out of the Theological Department of Baylor University in Waco, Texas, and received its charter as an independent organization in 1908. Two years later its Board accepted an offer of land for the campus and funds for its first building from the citizens of Fort Worth. The two-hundred acre area was on the highest natural elevation in Tarrant County and came to be known as "Seminary Hill." The first building was named "Fort Worth Hall" in honor of the school's community.

But Dr. Aulick didn't stop at sound advice. He was also instrumental in finding a place for them to live and a church for them to pastor. A former student, now working on a doctorate at Southwestern, would be vacating both a house and a pulpit. Dr. Aulick recommended his protégé to replace him. Benjamin was duly invited to preach in a revival at the Baptist church in Myra in view of a call, and took a bus there in the late summer. The next Saturday the church voted to invite him as pastor, and he returned home with work and housing secured. Although the people at Ranchvale were sad to see them go, they sent them off with their blessing, as well as some practical help. Albert Matlock offered to make their seventy-five-dollar per month car payments for several months and Wendell Madera moved their belongings, including La Nell's large upright piano, to their new lodgings in his truck.

No accident befell either the truck with their earthly possessions or the 1947 Plymouth they had bought new the year before to replace their old clunker. As Benjamin and La Nell sped down the highway to Fort Worth, they talked over their immediate future. The idea was for Benjamin to earn a Bachelor of Divinity, which would put him on the fast track to a Doctorate in Theology, while La Nell worked on a Master's in Religious Education. Then they would be ready for full-time teaching and preaching. It looked like plain sailing.

Cowtown

"Pastor Bedford?" asked a lady's voice. "I'm calling on behalf of the Deacon Board of the Muenster Baptist Church. We attended the revival you preached at Myra, and the church has voted to call you as pastor."

"I will be in Myra on Sunday. Perhaps we could meet there," suggested a bemused Benjamin from the Seminary switchboard. He and La Nell had not finished unpacking and did even not have their own phone yet. They had now been approached by three churches in less than one month. The latest invitation was somewhat more understandable than the interest shown by a little church in Heidenheimer on the recommendation of someone who had attended that same revival. The tiny rural community was located in Bell County, one hundred twenty-seven miles southeast of Fort Worth. The proposed contact had been declined with thanks.

The other two congregations, however, came to a mutually beneficial agreement. Benjamin would pastor both churches, alternating Sundays between them, and the congregations would take turns hosting and visiting each other. The two towns were only five miles apart, approximately eighty miles north of Fort Worth in western Cooke County. Myra, named after the daughter of the superintendent who built the railroad along which it grew, was the site of one of the first oil wells drilled in the county but it soon went dry and the congregation of around seventy consisted largely of retired people, farmers and schoolteachers. Most of the men in Muenster's thirty-to-forty-member congregation, on the other hand, held jobs as oilfield workers and were considered to be at the lower end of the social scale by the local citizenry. Their town had been founded by German Catholic settlers Carl and Emil Flusche and had originally been called Westphalia but, since the name was already taken, it was renamed after the capital of that German region. More than ninety percent of the population was Catholic. On the Sundays they went to Myra it was just like going home to New Mexico, but when they went to Muenster it was like going to a foreign country.

According to Benjamin and La Nell's carefully planned budget, they needed fifty dollars per week to cover their expenses. Each of the churches paid thirty-five dollars every other week, leaving them fifteen dollars short. Benjamin talked to Safeway's general manager in Fort Worth, who agreed to hire him to work only the hours required to reach that amount. The standard pay was eight-five cents per hour but went up to one dollar when he worked in the meat market.

Fort Worth's slogan is "Where the West Begins," with good reason. Geographically, it is set in the Cross Timbers region, the boundary between the more heavily forested eastern regions and the almost treeless Great Plains. It is part of the Cross Timbers' Grand Prairie ecoregion and has a humid subtropical climate. A treaty signed with the Native Americans in the mid-nineteenth century provided that they were to remain west of the future site of the city, and the area past this line became known as "where the west began." Fort Worth, established in 1849 as an Army outpost on a bluff overlooking the Trinity River, was named for Major General William Jenkins Worth, second-in-command during the Mexican American War. Its first nickname was "Cowtown," earned as it grew from a stop in the cattle drives along the legendary Old Chisholm Trail to a center of the cattle and ranching industries. The second nickname was "Panther City," a scornful epithet resulting from an article published in the Dallas Herald in 1875 that described the decimation of the population due to the economic disaster that took place in the aftermath of the Civil War, the Reconstruction and the hard winter of 1873. According to the former Fort Worth attorney who had written the piece, the town had become so drowsy that he had seen a panther asleep in the street by the courthouse. The town embraced the name as it made its economic comeback in 1876; the "panther" motif is still popular among local businesses and organizations, and the Fort Worth police badge proudly displays a panther on top. The Texas & Pacific Railways arrived and with it a financial boom. The Fort Worth Stockyard became a premier cattle industry and the center of a large-scale wholesale trade. It began to be called the "Queen City of the Prairie" as it became the regional center of the transportation network, the westernmost railhead and transit point for cattle shipping. By 1900 it was one of the world's largest cattle markets. The population tripled between 1900 and 1910, and new activities were added: meat-packing, flour-milling, grain storage, oil, aircraft plants and military bases. They were followed by a cultural flowering, and the city became enriched with universities, museums, art galleries, theaters and a botanic garden.

For the first time in their lives, Benjamin and La Nell lived in a real city. Their new housing, however, was definitely a step down from the comfortable country parsonage at Ranchvale. It was a duplex with three rooms in a row (living room, kitchen and bedroom) and a bathroom that they shared with the other tenants. On the positive side, it was located at Frazier and Boyce, diagonally across from the Seminary's new Price Christian Education Building.

And, of course, studying was the reason they were there. They found that the strict standards at Eastern New Mexico had been the perfect training for their work at the Seminary. They placed out of most of the beginning courses and were thus able to take a greater and more varied number of advanced classes. The 96-100 points required for an "A" that their classmates groaned about were nothing new to them. Countless papers were churned out on Benjamin's trusty old Royal manual typewriter that someone had given him in high school and that he had first used to type his sermons for church and papers for school. Now that he had La Nell's expert typing and editing services at his disposal, he turned out increasingly polished work.

Although he didn't have a class with the Seminary's President until the next year, Benjamin saw him almost immediately after arriving in Fort Worth, when Dr. Head grasped his hand and exclaimed, "I wondered what had happened to those two boys from New Mexico. It's good to see you here!"

And Baby Makes Three

"Where is my baby?!" La Nell asked yet another nurse who rushed past her.

"We'll get him to you real soon, honey," chirped the nurse breezily with a bright artificial smile.

The baby had been born shortly after midnight and, although it was a natural childbirth, the then standard procedure of "knock-'em-out, drag-'em-out obstetrics" had been followed, which called for sedating the mother and delivering the baby with forceps. When La Nell regained consciousness, she was told that the baby had been taken to the nursery to be weighed, measured and cleaned up. It was Sunday and Benjamin had had to rush off early in order to make the two-hour drive to Myra in time for church. Over twelve hours passed with no sign of the baby. The only information imparted to the new mother was that the hospital was having a busy day and that the baby would be brought "soon." La Nell began to imagine all too vividly what might be wrong.

Meanwhile, it dawned on the congregation in Myra that it might be a good thing for the new father to be with his wife and baby on this momentous occasion, so they cancelled the evening service and sent him home. When Benjamin arrived at the hospital, he found La Nell busily counting fingers and toes, and going over every inch of their newborn. He was a beautiful, perfect six-pound baby—the hospital staff had simply been "too busy" to reunite him with his mother.

So far, the whole process of having a baby had been full of unexpected twists and turns. As soon as they had settled into their new routine of school, church and supermarket work, La Nell and Benjamin decided to start spreading their family tent. They were somewhat startled to discover that La Nell was already pregnant by October, but that promised to work out well, since the baby would be born in the summer, right between semesters. The doctor had promised to keep a close eye on La Nell knowing that her blood type was O negative while Ben's was A positive, and reassured them that incompatibility was seldom a problem during the first pregnancy. What they didn't count on was La Nell's violent morning sickness that finally forced her to drop out of school in the middle of the spring semester. Benjamin did not go to summer school, but worked full time for Safeway covering other people's vacations mainly as assistant manager, which often meant closing up at night. Nevertheless, he also did quite a bit of extra preaching in revivals, one of which was in Martin, near the New Mexico border. La Nell took the opportunity to pay a quick visit to her mother in Portales while Benjamin preached, right after they were taken for a spin on their first airplane ride in a small twin-engine aircraft belonging to one of the deacons.

The Saturday before the baby was born, La Nell began to have contractions. She and Benjamin walked for hours and even played miniature golf until she felt it was time to go to the hospital. Instead of the sympathetic welcome she expected, La Nell was met with open skepticism and a maddeningly condescending "Now, dearie, you're still way too small. Go home and relax. You can come back to see the doctor on Monday, during office hours." But, since the contractions were exceedingly real, La Nell insisted on being admitted and the receptionist finally decided to humor her, rolling her eyes in a manner that said all too clearly, "We'll see about this!"

David Allen Bedford was born at 1:09 a.m. on Sunday, July 24, 1949 at All Saints Hospital. Because he was the first baby born that week, he received a large basket overflowing with baby products. Two generous showers had left the Bedford nursery well stocked and had allowed them to buy a handsome crib and Babee Tenda safety table that would serve for all of their little ones.

In spite of coming from very large families, no relatives were near enough to be with them to welcome the baby. Mother Watson had taken a full-time job as house-mother for the twelve-year-old girls at the Children's Home when Tom started college and could not leave, but Mother Bedford came right away to cook and clean for a couple of weeks while La Nell recovered her strength. She was going to need it because the pace became more hectic than ever.

Benjamin and La Nell usually left for Myra or Muenster on Friday and returned on Monday. A tornado had demolished the Baptist church building in Myra and it had been replaced by a handsome new structure, but there was no parsonage either there or at Muenster, so several of the church families took turns putting them up. Their most frequent hosts by far were Fred and Ruby McTaggart in Myra and the Lawsons in Muenster. The McTaggarts lived in a small house behind the church building and usually put the Bedfords in their comfortable little den, which even boasted a television. The "Macs'" generous hospitality soon turned into a determined protectiveness, especially after the baby was born. They assumed the role of foster grandparents and claimed babysitting privileges whenever they considered that the Bedfords would be going into an "unsuitable" atmosphere. David fully reciprocated their affection.

When Benjamin had to work at Safeway on Saturday or Monday, they went back and forth from Fort Worth on Sunday. An unexpected stroke of luck was that the crib mattress fit exactly into the back seat space, so the baby could rest in comfort on the two-hour trips. The trunk was usually crammed with delicious farm fare that the Bedfords shared with their less fortunate classmates and neighbors. Occasionally Benjamin worked from midnight to seven a.m. and went straight to class at 8:00. On the nights that La Nell stayed up typing Benjamin's papers up into the wee hours, he would see to feeding and changing the baby during the night so that she could grab a few hours of uninterrupted sleep and make it through the next day. Benjamin could practically perform these parenting duties with his eyes closed. One night it was borne in upon him that mechanical action was not quite enough when he woke up to find himself in the kitchen, all set to pour alcohol onto the butter rather than milk into the bottle. While La Nell was in class David stayed at the Seminary nursery, where he was quite a favorite. He became famous for the little straw hat that he refused to take off even at naptime. It was a gift from the McTaggarts, who got it for him when they saw how much he loved Fred's.

Meanwhile, all the way from New Mexico Mother Watson prayed them from school to church and back. She could not rest until they had arrived safely at their destination. They did not phone because they could not afford the long-distance calls; nevertheless, she "just knew" when they were safe and she could go to sleep.

Bright Eyes

"I'm afraid we can't hold off on the tonsillectomy any longer," the doctor told the Bedfords when their little son was eight months old. David was an extremely bright baby with fair hair and sparkly brown eyes. At six months he had exclaimed, "See the lights!" upon seeing his first Christmas tree. One month later mouths hung open in the doctor's waiting room, and the nurse who had whisked him away from his mother to have an infected arm lanced nearly dropped him, when he complained, "I want my mommy!" At around the same time he started pulling himself up and walking around the crib. He behaved beautifully and would have been incredibly easy to care for had it not been for the frequent bouts of high fever he began having at two or three months of age.

Following one particularly high fever, his parents noticed a sudden drop in his physical liveliness. After falling straight back a couple of times and knocking himself out, he lost his confidence and no longer attempted to walk on his own. For a long time after that he had to have his hand held. Then he progressed to holding onto just one finger and from there to literally grasping at straws. Benjamin would take a straw from the broom and, while he held one end and David the other, everything was fine. Eventually the day arrived when they were able to dispense with the straw.

La Nell had vivid memories of the agonies that her younger brother Thomas suffered as a child from infected tonsils that poisoned his entire system. She remembered her parents holding him as he convulsed and screamed that they were trying to kill him, so she was easily convinced to have the surgery performed. The problem was paying for it. After talking it over, Benjamin and La Nell decided that, rather than postpone the operation, they would use the money they had set aside for the upcoming rent and utilities and take out a loan from the Seminary to pay the household bills.

The Post Office was on the way to the hospital and they stopped a moment to check on their mail. There was only one envelope, postmarked in Ranchvale. It was from Willard O'Rear, who had been active in their youth group there. He wrote: "Dear Pastor Bedford, I sold some cattle and wheat and felt like making a special offering apart from the tithe. After praying, I decided to divide it between Foreign Missions and you. Lord bless, Willard." Enclosed was a check for the exact amount, down to the penny, required for the surgery and medicine.

The operation was a success and David soon felt much better. Mother Watson finally got some days off and made straight for Fort Worth to spend time with her newest grandchild She fell for him like a ton of bricks and called him her "Bright Eyes." In spite of their natural affinity, they didn't always understand each other. One evening while she was preparing dinner David sat down on the floor near her, opened a cabinet, pulled out pots, pans and lids, and began playing percussion. Startled, his grandmother took them away and put them up. To her astonishment, he took them out again and looked pitifully hurt when she scolded him. Later that night she found out that La Nell always let him play with those pots and pans when she worked in the kitchen.

David's arrival was a big event for the extended Bedford family. Although Benjamin was the youngest of six brothers, he was the first of them to have a boy. Everyone was eager to see him. When Mary went to visit L.D. in Odessa, they decided to take a family party to Fort Worth. L.D. filled up his car with his wife, Mary and three of David's cousins: Carla, La Dee and Frankie. They arrived only to find that Benjamin was gone, preaching at a revival in Ward's Chapel, Oklahoma, so they decided to join him there. Billie led the way in her car while L.D. drove La Nell and David in their Plymouth. Billie took the lack of a speed limit seriously and L.D. had to keep the pedal to the metal to keep up with her. The tiny church could not afford to cover the Bedford's travel expenses, but the generous congregation loaded down their car with delicious fruits and vegetables.

Influential Professors

"These are the sorriest papers I have ever seen," Dr. Earl Guinn informed the one hundred and twenty students in his preaching class gloomily. "Ninety to one hundred is an A, eighty to ninety is a B and seventy to eighty is a C. Beyond that, I can't help you!" Benjamin breathed a sigh of relief as he saw his own ninety-six—he had "read" the professor correctly. In spite of his sometimes eccentric behavior, Dr. Guinn was an excellent teacher, and many of his sayings stuck with his students forever, such as: "When I was in college I won a horseshoe throwing contest, but it hasn't helped me any in my ministry!" Benjamin remembered this story six years later when he received his own horseshoe throwing trophy at a Family Camp in Glorieta, and didn't let it go to his head.

The President of the Seminary, Dr. Head, taught Evangelism. Besides being one of the most intellectually brilliant scholars of the time, he was also the humblest of men. He taught his students that evangelism concerned not only theology and message, but the guidance of the Holy Spirit. The class met two times per week, and on the Friday session he had them think of someone to contact over the next weekend. Then he instructed them to pray for those people and for each other. The first Friday he did this, Benjamin overheard a classmate snicker, "Looks like the old man ran out of juice so he's having a prayer meeting." But in Benjamin's own experience, this led directly to the conversion of two older couples, one in each of his churches. He baptized them all in Myra because there was no baptistry in Muenster.

Dr. Cal Guy had been named to the George and Ida Bottoms Chair of Missions in 1948. He was the successor of Frank Means and Baker James Cauthen, both of whom went on to have influential ministries at the Foreign Mission Board, the former as Director for Latin America and the latter as Executive Secretary. Dr. Guy founded the School of Missions and had tremendous influence across denominational lines. He emphasized the need to contextualize the teaching of the Gospel in the culture of those who heard it, as well as the importance of including and promoting national participation in the ministry as a means of passing from collaboration to autonomy. He encouraged his students to forget about prestigious denominational positions and focus on the nitty-gritty: "Here at Southwestern, we are the ones who chop wood and carry water." In no small part due to his spiritual leadership, this Seminary soon became the Southern Baptists' main source of new missionaries.

Another groundbreaking professor at this time was J.M. Price, who was the primary promoter of Christian Education in the Convention. He led Southwestern in pioneering the first School of Religious Education. The school's building, later named after him, was under construction at the time, right across the street from where La Nell and Benjamin lived. The other Religious Education professor, Dr. W.L. House, later went to the Convention's Sunday School Board and headed the emphasis on Religious Education in literature.

New Testament and Greek were taught by Ray Summers, Jack McGorman and Curtis Vaughn. Dr. Summers, who would become the youngest director and then dean of the School of Theology, was an extremely handsome and pleasant man. In one of his classes he had divided the students into groups, one of which was headed by Benjamin, to prepare presentations. Dr. Summers was walking among them, smiling benevolently, when he suddenly asked, "Is Benjamin Bedford here?" Upon catching sight of him, he added, "I bring greetings for Benjamin and La Nell from New Mexico." He had just returned from the State BSU Convention, where he had been the guest speaker. When he was an upperclassman at the Seminary, Benjamin became Dr. Summer's grader.

In fact, the faculty included an amazing group of dedicated scholars, teachers and writers. Old Testament and Hebrew were taught by Professors Leslie Carlson, Robert Daniels and Ralph Smith. Church History was the field of H.E. Barnes, Robert Baker and W.R. Estep, with whose daughter David was to have his first date years later, on his parents' second furlough. Professors Newman and John Newport taught Philosophy, while Professors J.J. Northcutt, Charles Trentham and Leo Garrett, all prolific writers, taught Theology, and T.B. Maston and C.H. Scutter taught Ethics.

Benjamin and La Nell placed out of quite a few classes because of their excellent preparation in college under Drs. Aulick and Humphreys. Many of their classmates were working on doctorates and the academic standard was high. The advanced classes required long hours of reading and studying, as well as preparing a great number of in-depth papers. Because their classes were so large and their schedules so hectic, most of the people they knew at the Seminary either sat beside them in class, lived nearby or pastored churches in the same association. Years later, during one of their furloughs, they met H.W. Bartlett at a School of Missions in Artesia to which Benjamin was invited through one of his former New Mexico deacons. They discovered that they had graduated from Southwestern at the same time and, because of the alphabetical proximity of their names, had probably been seated only two or three chairs apart at the ceremony.

Far Afield

"We usually recommend pastoring for a few years after the Seminary before going on the field but, given the experience you already have and the urgent need in Argentina at this time, we would like for you to consider going as soon as you graduate," said Mary Francis Dawkins, Associate Personnel Director of the Southern Baptist Foreign Mission Board, or FMB for short.

Benjamin had always felt a tug toward missions. He had spent a good many of his formative years in a church with a strong emphasis on evangelism and missions. The First Baptist Church of Clovis had sent out three of its own as missionaries to Brazil in the forties, Barney Foreman and the two Buster sisters. It provided a thriving Training Union Program and plenty of practical opportunities for service. Benjamin had worked alongside a home missionary, Edith Mims, at the church's Spanish Mission and had heard his first foreign missionary speaker during a youth camp at Inlow Baptist Camp in the beautiful Manzano Mountains of Central New Mexico. This was Martha Ellis, who told them about her work with the very active Women's Missionary Union in Argentina.

But it was not until a strange confluence of events took place that Benjamin and La Nell began to give serious consideration to becoming foreign missionaries. When David was three months old, La Nell had taken him to Portales on the bus to visit her mother and show him off. While she was there, she had browsed through her beloved Campus Bookstore and picked up a volume on how to learn to speak Spanish. At that very moment, back in Fort Worth, Benjamin was in the Chapel listening as Cal Guy spoke at Missions Day, a special event sponsored by the Seminary every semester. This time, the tug turned into an overwhelming urge. Evidently many of his classmates felt the same way, because over three hundred of the one thousand thirty-five students enrolled in that fall semester of 1949 declared their intention to go into foreign mission service.

As soon as La Nell returned, Benjamin told her how strongly he felt. She, in turn, showed him the book she had bought and recounted her own sudden urge to learn Spanish. They both knew it was time to take practical steps. Over the next few months, they contacted the Foreign Mission Board and were sent information and invited to fill out forms that called for detailed descriptions of their lives, their beliefs and their experience. This eventually led to an on-campus interview with a representative of the FMB, who told them that the Board had been amazed at the experience that Benjamin had managed to accumulate by the ripe old age of twenty-four. That was what had prompted the proposal for immediate action.

Benjamin and La Nell exchanged glances. He had already applied for graduate school at Southwestern. The Cook County Association had asked Benjamin to consider living in Gainesville and working as part-time associational missionary while he completed his doctorate and La Nell finished her Master's degree. They had been thinking of going to the mission field after that, with their degrees and some missionary experience already under their belts.

"But Argentina needs you right away! Most of the missionaries there are about to retire. If you go now, we'll give you a half-year extension on one of your furloughs to finish your studies," countered Ms. Dawkins.

So La Nell and Benjamin embarked on the series of interviews and examinations required before the Foreign Mission Board could make its final decision to appoint them, and they began to find out everything they could about Argentina. They invited missionaries passing through Fort Worth to visit them and tell them all about the country, its people and their work. One of these was Vada Waldron, a charming single middle-aged lady who worked with kindergarten and preschool children in Mendoza, in the foothills of the Andes, not far from the highest peak in the Western Hemisphere, and another was Leroy David, who taught at the Bible Institute in Córdoba, in the very heart of Argentina. They invited them to lunch at the same time, but Mr. David felt that separate visits would be more appropriate, in order not to give rise to any misunderstandings, given his status as a widower. Dr. Guy assigned them research projects on Argentina in the special Missions class for prospective missionaries and read them information on the new facilities that were being built for the Seminary in the capital city, Buenos Aires.

The final interview was scheduled to take place at the Foreign Mission Board's headquarters in Richmond, Virginia in April 1951, shortly before graduation. First they had to undergo standard physical and psychological exams right there in Fort Worth. This was their first experience with a psychologist. He had a short, friendly chat with Benjamin and then proceeded to rake La Nell over the coals, in an apparent attempt to discover whether or not an adolescent experience had left her with a persecution complex. La Nell had dated several boys very casually when she was in high school. One of them wanted a more serious relationship and hounded her about it until she felt forced to tell him in no uncertain terms, "If you and I were the last people left on earth, there would be smoke going up two chimneys!" When she missed class for several weeks due to appendicitis, the young man had carried out a smear campaign in an attempt to set the other students against her. She had never imagined that this would prove so fascinating to a psychologist.

Leonard and Daisy arrived in Fort Worth at about that time. Of course the friends got together, and the Bedfords discovered that the Lanes were in town for their own FMB exams and were seeking appointment as missionaries to Africa, possibly in Nigeria. Like Golden Gate, Southwestern treated missionary candidates with special consideration and granted them the time to make the trip to Richmond and juggle test dates and paper deadlines. Benjamin was supposed to grade final exams for Dr. Summers that week and offered to do it when he returned, but the professor answered, "That's O.K. I'll just have Hoke Smith grade them all," so he left it to his fellow grader and future missionary with a clear conscience.

Mother Watson was visiting and arranged to take David back to New Mexico with her so they could go about their business knowing that he was receiving the best loving care. Of course David, who was still three months short of his second birthday, didn't really understand what was going on, but he was thrilled with the idea of riding the bus with Grandmother. When Benjamin got on to give his mother-in-law a last-minute message, David thought he was going to take him off and said, "No, no!" as he burrowed deeper into his grandmother's lap.

La Nell and Benjamin went to Richmond by train. Their classmates Don and Violet Orr, who were to be the first music missionaries ever appointed, travelled with them. Their childcare arrangements for Randy, who was several months younger than David, were ingenious, to say the least. Passengers were not allowed to get off the train until their final destination, but when the train made a cargo stop in Little Rock, Violet's mother was waiting on the platform and received her grandson and his bag through the carriage window, to be picked up on the return trip.

Farewell to Home and Family

"Well, this is truly epic-making," exclaimed exhausted Personnel Secretary Samuel E. Maddox. "It was harder for Charles to make up his mind than for Truman to decide to fire MacArthur!" President Harry Truman had finally relieved General Douglas MacArthur as commander of the U.S. forces fighting the Korean War on April 11, the day after the Foreign Mission Board formally appointed the newest group of missionaries. Charles Clark, one of the Bedford's closest friends, had found it difficult to decide between Venezuela and Argentina, but finally came down on the side of the Caribbean nation.

It had been an intense week. First the prospective missionaries were placed into one of three geographical groups—Africa, Latin America or the Orient—and had a series of in-depth meetings with a committee consisting of the Area Secretary, in Benjamin and La Nell's case Everett Gill, and several members of the Board. They were asked seemingly endless questions about why they wanted to be missionaries, their beliefs and their theology, and they were assisted in choosing a specific country of the region in which they would be serving. After the area committee recommended the candidates, they were examined and voted upon by the entire Board. At that point, they were appointed and commissioned with an inspiring message by the Executive Director, M.T. Rankin, a distinguished former missionary to China. Of their special friends, the Lanes were appointed to Nigeria, the Clarks to Venezuela and the Orrs to Colombia, while Benjamin and La Nell were both appointed as evangelistic field missionaries to Argentina. Their sole country-specific orientation consisted of informal chats with missionaries Quarrels and Fowler.

Along with the rest of their fellow candidates, the Bedfords were staying at a hotel and managed to squeeze in some sightseeing in that historical area. Richmond itself was beautiful, with its stately buildings along broad avenues lined with cherry trees in full bloom. They even went to Congress in Washington, D.C., where Don Orr and Dub Johnson met with Texas Senator Lyndon B. Johnson to request his assistance in getting them released from the Reserves so they could go to the mission field.

Before leaving, they sat down with the Area Secretary to hammer out their schedule. By the last week of July they would be in San José, Costa Rica to begin a year of intensive language study. Between then and graduation at the end of May, they needed to wind up all of their Stateside affairs, say their good-byes to family, friends and church, and give their testimonies on the East Coast at Ridgecrest and on the West Coast at the Southern Baptist Convention in San Francisco, California. Meanwhile, the Board would get cracking on the paperwork for their passports and visas.

By the time they got home, it had been nearly two weeks since Mother Watson had taken David and his parents were getting frantic to see him. Billie and Marion had offered to return him to Fort Worth, but they didn't show up on the night they were expected and there was no word on their whereabouts. The next morning they appeared at the door bright and early: they had gotten into town late the night before and, rather than disturb them at that hour, they had checked into a nearby hotel, unaware that the anxious parents had been unable to sleep a wink. Billie and Marion stayed and accompanied them on the weekend activities in Myra. David did not want to be parted from his mother and father for a moment, but every time their eyes met his parents encountered a wounded look that clearly asked, "How could you leave me so long?" and pierced them right through the heart.

Finals and Benjamin's graduation went by in a blur. They had to vacate their apartment at the end of May and, except for David's crib and Babee Tenda, they sold most of their belongings, including La Nell's piano and the car. A Seminary student was interested in the vehicle and traded cars with them while he went to Wichita Falls to get the loan approved. When he returned they swapped back until the paperwork went through. As David climbed in the car his family had had his entire life, he ran his hand over it lovingly and sighed, "I like this car!"

The Bedfords lived on what was left of the proceeds from the sales after squaring away all of their bills, since July would be the first month that they would be employees of the Foreign Mission Board. The church at Muenster rented them a little house for two weeks while they led a Vacation Bible School and a revival. Then they took their leave of the congregations at Myra and Muenster, and took a bus to New Mexico.

Mother Watson's home in Portales became the base for their last month in the U.S. They caught up on David's doings while he had stayed with his grandmother.

"By the way, we meant to ask you how you taught David to drink from a Coke bottle."

"Teach him? I didn't. He asked for a Coke and I gave him one. He drank it like he'd been doing it all of his life. I'll tell you what got to me, though. See that picture I have of the two of you? He would hold it and look at it, and then smile with tears running down his cheeks." It got to them, too, and they were glad there would be no more separations.

There were still two trips the three of them had to take before leaving the country. The first was to Ridgecrest Baptist Camp. They rode a train to Asheville, North Carolina and took in the views of the lush Smoky and Blue Ridge Mountains. David wanted sunglasses like his parents', so they got him a pair in red plastic and knocked out the lenses: he was all set for the summer in shorts, T-shirt and "glasses."

The second trip involved another train ride, this time to Los Angeles, where La Nell's brother W.L. and his wife Ola picked them up and drove them to the Baptist Convention in San Francisco. They sat with David while his parents gave their testimonies and then enjoyed showing them around some of the California sights. They went to Nob Hill, Alcatraz, the Seal Rocks and the Golden Gate Bridge. A special treat was getting to see their old mentor, now teaching at Golden Gate Seminary. Dr. Aulick kept looking at their little family and beaming with pride and affection. They went up and down California, visiting the Sequoia National Forest and Knotts Berry Farm.

They also got to see a lot of relatives. All of La Nell's older brothers except Kenneth, who farmed in West Texas, now lived in California. W.L. and John had gotten jobs with Firestone making tires and were both very active in church. John was a deacon and W.L. had become a pastor. He had gotten his degree at California Baptist College while he worked and preached. He eventually started three thriving churches in the Los Angeles area. On the Bedford side, all of Benjamin's siblings except for Billie and L.D. had also moved to California. Mother Bedford was there visiting children and grandchildren, and returned to Clovis on the train with Benjamin and his family.

Now the clock was really ticking. The Baptists of Portales organized a reception for them at the Children's Home which fell on the evening of the day Benjamin had his wisdom teeth extracted. La Nell's sister La Wanna and Herbert were back in Ranchvale, expecting their third child. The church wanted Benjamin to preach there on their last Sunday in the States. They had to be in New Orleans on Monday and, since they couldn't be at the services in Ranchvale and catch the train on time, the church paid the difference for them to fly out on a DC3 from the Clovis Air Base.

They packed two suitcases each, mainly with clothes, books and toys. They were leaving with the blessing of their families, friends and churches. The final seal of approval and confirmation was Mother Watson finally telling La Nell about the night that she had nearly died at the age of three and God had answered her mother's prayers and saved her, but had made her understand that she had to be willing to let her daughter serve Him far away.

Do You Know the Way to San José?

There were two overnight stops on the way to Costa Rica. The first was in New Orleans, where the Bedfords had only a fleeting glimpse of the exotic French Quarter as they rushed through the process of getting their visas at the Costa Rican Consulate. They met up with the Clarks and made the rest of the trip together. Since San José was not equipped to receive large commercial aircraft, they flew from New Orleans to Guatemala City. During their first night in Latin America what struck them the most was how different everything smelled. A small plane took them on the last leg of the trip, and the resident missionaries were waiting for them at the airport to help them settle into their new living quarters.

The Bedfords were taken to a house on *Calle Cuatro*—Fourth Street. Although it was hardly in a prime location, being near a prison, it was the largest house they had ever lived in. The all-brick construction was new to them, but the really incredible part was that it actually had servants' quarters, already occupied by two young women, one to help with the housework and one to be David's nanny. Unfortunately, they did not speak English and the Bedfords did not speak Spanish.

"Don't worry about it," said their hosts confidently. "We'll tell them how you want things done and, if you have any trouble, just call us on the phone and we'll translate for you."

The very next day La Nell took them up on this offer: 'We just got home and found our clothes strewn all over the ground in the back yard! What do you think that means?!"

"Ha, ha! It's nothing—that's just the way they usually dry clothes."

There was quite a lot to get used to: the language, the climate, the food, the customs. They always knew when they had said something especially peculiar, because the maid would politely say "¿SeÑOR?" or "¿SeñoRA?," with the pitch rising on the last syllable. On one occasion, after noticing that María did the ironing on the table, Benjamin got an ironing board and set it up for her. Beaming, he meant to say, "*Es mejor, ¿verdad?*"[2] but what he actually said was, "*Es mujer, ¿verdad?*"[3]

"¿SeÑOR?"

Soon it was La Nell's turn. She decided that she would like to try making tomato juice—*jugo de tomate*—but what she actually said was, "*Quiero hacer juicio de tomate.*"[4]

"¿SeñoRA?"

The food was different: heavy on rice, beans and tropical fruit. Regardless of how well they washed the vegetables, practically everyone suffered from amoebas. In fact, David was the only missionary child that did not get them. It was apparent that he had not quite gotten over their unexpectedly long separation during the appointment process, because at first he cried heartbreakingly when his parents left for class in the morning, but he soon fell into the new routine and enjoyed the time he spent with his nanny. She adored him, although she was a little concerned the first time he insisted on setting a place at the table for his imaginary friend "Boy."

The tropical climate was a decided change from the extreme hot and cold dry weather of the High Plains. Although the humidity took some getting used to, the Bedfords soon discovered that, unlike Texas and New Mexico, the weather in Costa Rica is supremely dependable. The year is divided into two seasons, defined by rainfall: the dry season, from December to April, is called "summer" and the rainy season, from May to November, is called "winter" and coincides with the Atlantic hurricane season, but fortunately the path of the storms is further north.

---

[2] "Better, isn't it?
[3] "You're a woman, aren't you?
[4] "I want to make tomato judgment."

The country has several microclimates that depend on elevation, rainfall and topography. San José, in the heart of the central plateau, is 1161 meters[5] above sea level, with an average temperature of 25°C[6] and an annual precipitation of 1800 millimeters,[7] more than 90% of which falls during the rainy season. People arrange their outings around the rain, which falls a little earlier and a little longer as the season advances, and, thanks to the marvelous drainage system, the streets are clean and clear as soon as the rain stops.

However, the Bedfords were not there to sightsee but to study Spanish.

---

[5] 3809 feet
[6] 77°F
[7] 70.8 inches

Tongue Twister

"Cinco horas al día"[8] was the motto that the Spanish Language Institute drilled into their students. It was even set to music for them to sing. They were expected to complete five hours of class and five hours of practice every day. The Bedfords got up early every morning and took a twenty-minute bus ride to get started on this onerous schedule by 8:00 sharp.

The Institute had been founded by the United Presbyterian Board in Colombia in 1942 and had moved to San José in 1950. Under the direction of Dr. and Mrs. Otto La Porte, the school taught missionaries of all denominations headed for Spanish-speaking countries. As soon as they arrived, the students underwent placement tests and were assigned to evenly-matched groups, each of which had four students. La Nell was found to have outstanding language aptitude and was placed in the most advanced group, together with Don Orr, Shirley Clark and a woman from the Church of Christ Mission. Benjamin was in the "spouses' group" since Charles Clark and the Pentecostal woman's husband were both in it.

There were four classes: grammar, phonetics and two rounds of conversation, with a lab for practice. Grammar was taught by Mrs. La Porte and phonetics by Anita Aguilar. Unfortunately, Mrs. La Porte had been unable to shed her American accent altogether and La Nell reproduced her pronunciation all too faithfully. *"No, no, ¡así no!"*[9] Anita would exclaim, without identifying the problem. It was Don Orr who figured it out: "The only thing you're doing wrong is 'gliding' the vowels." La Nell self-corrected and produced pure, steady Spanish vowels. Anita was in raptures and considered the

---

[8] "Five hours a day"
[9] "No, no, not like that!"

progress her own doing, proclaiming La Nell to be the best student she had ever had. Meanwhile, Mrs. La Porte gave Benjamin fits and the sinking feeling that he would never make it. For the first time they were faced with learning something at school that couldn't be mastered solely by applying their minds, and it was often frustrating.

There was an abundance of set phrases for mastering pronunciation that had to be repeated over and over again and became engraved in their brains forever:

"Los abuelos están en el agua"[10]

"Los dedos del doctor son delgados"[11]

"El hijo del rey va a la guerra"[12]

"R con R guitarra; R con R barril. Mira qué rápido corren las ruedas del ferrocarril"[13]

For most students, speaking was easier than understanding, but the reverse was true for Benjamin, who was outstanding in listening comprehension. The Bedfords even bought a copper wire recorder from a departing missionary, Reuben Frank, so they could practice their pronunciation at home. While they were concluding the transaction, David betrayed his heavy exposure to the King James Bible when he described his latest accident to their visitor: "I fainteth and I falleth and I bumpeth my head!"

They began working on very practical vocabulary straight away: how to buy items at the market, what to say at church and how to pray. It wasn't long before they had to put it all into practice. The Bedfords attended the *Primera Iglesia Bautista*.[14] whose pastor, Mr. Gutiérrez, laughed every time that La Nell spoke. At first she thought that her beginner's Spanish amused him, but it turned out that he just liked her and found her progress both surprising and delightful.

They were encouraged to participate from the very start, for example, by taking up the offering and serving as ushers. By the second quarter La Nell was given a women's Sunday School class

---

[10] "The grandparents are in the water"
[11] "The doctor's fingers are thin"
[12] "The king's son goes to war"
[13] "R plus R guitar; R plus R barrel. Rapidly run the wheels of the railroad"
[14] First Baptist Church

with the assistance of the pastor's wife. After preparing all week, she ran out of Spanish in about fifteen minutes and Mrs. Gutiérrez took over, but soon La Nell was able to make it all the way through and was left completely in charge. Benjamin had a similar experience with a junior boys' class at a mission point in Alajuela, which he reached by a thirty-to-forty-minute bus ride early every Sunday morning and where he worked his way up to teaching the entire forty-five minute class.

By the third quarter, the students who were pastors began writing sermons and preaching them to each other in class. Before long they were carrying out real speaking engagements in the churches, where language was not the only challenge. Charles Clark was concentrating very hard on his delivery at the Primera Iglesia Bautista and had just supported his point by quoting Jesus on the subject. As he took breath to continue, a drunk who had staggered in from the street and settled into one of the front pews popped up and exclaimed, "*Sí, bueno. ¿Pero qué dice San Pablo?*"[15]

---

[15] "Yes, all right. But what does St. Paul say?"

Coffee Beans and Volcanoes

Although he was only two years old, David played a major role in the Bedfords' social life. Of course they met a lot of people while they were in Costa Rica, including several missionaries who were finishing their last quarter of language study before leaving for Argentina—the Robertsons, Watsons, Coburns and Hollingsworths—and they spent a good part of the day with their group mates. But their best friends in Costa Rica were the Orrs and the Clarks, mainly because of the time they spent together so that David could be with Randy and Judy.

While David and Randy were busy with their toys, their parents played endless games of Rook over coffee and cake until it was time to take the last bus home. Don Orr was responsible for Benjamin's name undergoing its final transformation: "If I call my wife Vi, I'm sure not going to call you Benjamin!" He insisted on calling him "Ben." Soon everyone was following his lead, even, last but not least, La Nell.

The relationship with Judy proved how resourceful a person in love can be. One day at school Shirley Clark mentioned in passing something amusing that David had said.

"When did he say that?" La Nell wanted to know.

"Oh, sometime last week at our house."

"At your *house*?!"

"Yes, of course, although I'm not sure exactly when. After all, the niñera[16] takes him there to play with Judy practically every morning."

Aghast, La Nell asked the niñera if she had been taking David to the Clark's house every morning.

"Todas las mañanas David me da dinero para el autobús y me dice que se lo dio el papá."[17]

Sure enough, a daily morning ritual had developed in which David would ask his parents for a coin before they left for school. If they gave him a big one, he would ask for a little one, too, and if he got a little one first, he would ask for a big one, too. After they left, he would go to his nanny with the coins and tell her his daddy had given him bus money. He had figured out that those two coins were enough for them to ride one way and walk the other to and from Judy's house.

The friends also went together on the Saturday excursions organized to help the hard-working students relax. Costa Rica is ideal for sightseeing because of its small size and amazing variety. It is the second smallest Central American country, bordering on Nicaragua to the north and Panama to the south. It has 1061 kilometers[18] of coastline on the Pacific side and 212 kilometers[19] on the Caribbean-Atlantic side, with a jagged series of mountains and volcanoes along the Andean-Sierra Madre chain that runs throughout the Americas, as well as a fertile central plateau. At its narrowest, Costa Rica is only 119 kilometers[20] wide, and it is the only country in which both oceans can be seen from the same vantage point. In addition, it is the country with the greatest density of species in the world. There are big cats and tapirs, four species of monkeys, sloths, and a wide variety of birds and reptiles, to say nothing of the flora. Seven hundred species of birds and one hundred species of mammals have been identified there.

One of their most memorable outings was to the Ojo de Agua Water Park, whose natural spring spills out at a rate of 359 liters of

---

[16] Nanny
[17] "Every morning David gives me bus money and tells me that his daddy gave it to him."
[18] 631 miles
[19] 132 miles
[20] 74 miles

water per second,[21] and to the nearby Poás live volcano with blue water boiling in its depths. While Don Orr set up his tripod and his fancy camera, and made complicated calculations taking into account light and angles, Ben went up to the very edge of the crater, leaned over and snapped away with their trusty little Argus C3 rangefinder at what he hoped was the right setting. Much to Don's chagrin, Ben's amateurish efforts produced by far the most spectacular picture.

They also went to a coffee plantation and saw workers pick the beans by hand and place them in baskets tied in front. The beans were soaked in water to remove the husks and then spread out on the ground like gravel and stepped on for grinding. Ben got a good illustration for his sermons on Foreign Missions offerings out of it: one coffee bean doesn't make much coffee, but if you put a bunch of them together, it's a different story.

---

[21] Over 5,000 gallons per minute

Delayed

David also had a big impact on their relationship with the community. After three months, the Bedfords moved to a comfortable house on Calle Veinte,[22] near the market. It was in a nice part of town and had good neighbors. There was even a little girl to play with David. One day she was eying his little red rocking horse longingly and, while his full-time language student parents racked their brains for the appropriate way to tell her to get on and ride, their little stay-at-home son patted the saddle and said, "*¡Montate!*"[23]

David loved to sit on the low wall and watch the people walk down the street. He also liked to "preach" at the park, where he would stand on a corner telling Bible stories and singing, drawing delighted crowds. Soon everyone in San José knew the friendly little blond gringo. Even when they made their monthly trip to stock up at the market, the stall owners would ask, "*¿Ustedes son los padres de David?*"[24]

The Bedfords discovered that Costa Ricans not only loved children like all Latin Americans, but that they had to be among the nicest and most patient people on earth. They were always polite and helpful, never making fun of their linguistic limitations. In addition to the warmth and charm shared by Latin cultures, Costa Ricans have an independent and egalitarian outlook arising from their unique background. Costa Rica occupied an intermediate area, where the indigenous Mesoamerican and Andean populations

---

[22] Twentieth Street

[23] "Climb on" (Costa Ricans, like Argentines, use "*vos*" rather than "*tú*" for the informal second person)

[24] "Are you David's parents?"

overlapped, when the Spaniards arrived in the sixteenth century. The small native populations were almost wholly absorbed into the Spanish-speaking colonial society. Costa Rica became the southernmost province of the Captaincy General of Guatemala. The distance from the capital, the prohibition to trade to the south with Panama and the lack of desired resources (namely gold and silver) isolated it to such an extent that in 1719 one governor called it the poorest and most miserable Spanish colony in all of America. The country was ignored and left to develop on its own. Costa Rica did not even have to fight for its independence, because when Spain was defeated in the Mexican War of Independence, Guatemala declared the independence of all Central America, and from 1823 to 1839 Costa Rica was a province of the Federal Republic of Central America, which never had more than a very loose authority. Costa Rica felt little incentive for regional integration and declared itself sovereign.

Coffee was first grown in Costa Rica in the nineteenth century and began to be exported in 1843, becoming the main source of national wealth well into the next century. Most of it was grown in the Central Plateau and transported by oxcart to the Pacific port of Puntarenas. Since the main market was Europe, a transportation route to the Atlantic was essential. In the 1870s the government contracted a U.S. businessman, Minor Keith, to build a railroad to the Caribbean port of Limón which was completed in 1890. Most Afro-Costa Ricans are descendants of Jamaicans who sought railroad jobs. U.S. convicts and Chinese immigrants made up a good part of the remaining work force. The government granted Keith large tracts of land and a lease on the train route as payment. Bananas were produced on the land and exported to the U.S. They began to rival coffee as the main export and foreign-owned corporations (including the United Fruit Company) began to play a significant role in the country's economy.

Generally speaking, Costa Rica has been the most peaceful and stable Latin American country, with only two brief periods of violence. The first lasted from 1917 to 1919, at the end of which military dictator Federico Tinoco Granados was forced into exile, leading to the decline in size, wealth and political influence of the military. In 1948, José Figueres Ferrer led an armed uprising after a disputed presidential election. There were over two thousand casualties during the forty-four day Civil War. The victorious rebels formed a Junta that abolished the military altogether and oversaw the drafting of a new constitution by a democratically elected assembly and relinquished power on November 8, 1949. Figueres became a national hero and won the first democratic election under the new constitution in 1953, beginning an unbroken chain of peaceful and transparent democratically elected administrations.

The Bedfords arrived during this last transition period and, the longer they were there, the more they loved it and were even tempted to accept an invitation to stay and work in Guatemala. They did suffer one heartbreak, however. They had decided that it was about time to enlarge the family and La Nell was pregnant. On the only day Ben stayed in bed sick, with a bad ear infection, he was dragged out by an urgent call. La Nell was hemorrhaging and had been hospitalized. The RH factor had reared its ugly head and caused a miscarriage. For months afterwards she would find herself aimlessly opening and shutting drawers all over the house, driven by a powerful subconscious urge to find what had been lost.

When it was time for their group to leave for the respective assigned fields, they stayed behind because their residence papers for Argentina had not yet come through. Their good friends left and they moved into yet another house, temporarily vacated by furloughing missionaries and located in an even nicer neighborhood, near the university. Along with the house, they got the use of a Jeep, which made it a lot easier to get around.

While they waited for their resident visas, Ben took extra classes at the Institute and taught theology at the local Seminary, while La Nell continued to improve her Spanish through her church activities and daily conversation with the maids. Since only one permanent missionary family was left on the field, the Bedfords were pressed into service to receive the next big group of missionaries arriving for language school, help settle them in, counsel them and in general give them whatever support they needed. There were about fifteen couples and several single women—of whom the Ferrells, the Garners and Chris Eidson were assigned to Argentina—and they got to know them well. They were called upon to use every scrap of Spanish they knew in interpreting for them. It was especially necessary at first for Helen Goodrow, whose intensely southern Georgia accent defeated the meager

English of the Costa Ricans and caused Pastor Gutiérrez to exclaim, "¡Me mata!"[25]

They helped Bill and Opal Ferrell, and their little son Curtis, Southerners from Mississippi, move into the house vacated by the Clarks. While the Bedfords were showing them the ropes, the milkman and the man who delivered bread came by, wanting to know how much and how often to supply them. Everyone waited expectantly while the Ferrells stared at each other in silence. Finally, Ben broke the impasse and asked the men to come back the next day. Later, he and La Nell agreed: "They'll never make it "

At first glance, the Bedfords and the Ferrells had nothing in common but their vocation and little boys of the same age. But David and Curtis took matters out of their hands and brought them together during all outings because they were inseparable from the moment they met. It was the beginning of the most wonderful lifetime friendship of the two families.

---

[25] "She kills me!"

Bureaucracy 101

Argentine bureaucracy was no kinder or more thoughtful to the Bedfords than to anyone else. After four months of fruitless waiting for their visas in Costa Rica, the Foreign Mission Board decided that it was time to move forward regardless, and sent them home to take leave of their families and get their belongings ready for shipping.

Since five of their siblings were in the Los Angeles area, Ben and La Nell requested to be flown directly to California. They were given a tremendous send-off from San José with a farewell party and even a money tree that David kept trying to get his hands on. They had a huge family reunion in L.A. and got to meet the two newest additions to the Bedford clan—Jewel's daughter Linda and Ira's son Danny.

A little house was rented for them in Clovis on Eighth Street, right across from the Central Baptist Church, and they were able to visit their family and friends in the area. There were numerous speaking engagements and they were often lent vehicles to get there. One of these was the fanciest car they had ever seen, loaded with all of the latest features and gadgets, including automatic windows. Three-year-old David was absolutely fascinated and decided the same principle should apply to other things:

"Daddy, will you buy me a book that turns its own pages?"

"No, son, there aren't any books like that," laughed Ben, but he could tell that the little boy was by no means convinced.

There weren't many belongings to prepare. The Bedfords had received a list of recommended items to take to the field. Of these, they had decided to take a washing machine, a refrigerator and a stove. Their funds were not deep enough to cover everything, so they bought a beautiful new white Magic Chef gas range on credit, committing themselves to pay fifteen dollars per month for the next year. They packed pots and pans, dishes, flatware and glasses in a barrel. Among them was an elegant twelve-place set of China, a gift from the President of the First Baptist Church's Women's Missionary Union, whose thoughtfulness included allowing La Nell to choose the pattern. A selection of David's baby furniture and toys, a cedar chest, a sewing machine and books completed their earthly possessions.

When February arrived with no news, the Board decided that they had waited long enough. Reservations were made on a ship sailing from New York City in March and Dr. Gill told them, "If the visas have not arrived by then, you can get off in Montevideo and be missionaries there."

However, at what felt like the fifty-ninth minute of the eleventh hour, the long-awaited visas finally arrived, only to reveal that some of their information was no longer current since they had been made out as if they were still living in Costa Rica. After a frantic bout of telephoning, the Argentine consul in New Orleans graciously agreed to "fix" them, so Ben and David hopped on the next train and got the documents straightened out. The Consulate did not charge them, extending the courtesy of ministerial exemption.

When La Wanna discovered that they would be leaving from New York, she exclaimed, "Oh, you should try to get on 'Break the Bank'!" The last thing on Ben and La Nell's mind at that point was participating in a radio game show, but La Wanna sent for tickets anyway, and they arrived the very day they left Clovis.

The Bedfords had cashed in the small sum they had accumulated with the Annuity Board to buy a decent set of luggage. In one of the suitcases they packed David's beloved little record player so he could entertain himself with it on the long voyage. Unfortunately, the new bags proved to be tempting and the one with the record player in it was stolen. The railroad's insurance paid them one hundred dollars, with which they were able to replace the suitcases and clothes, but it was not enough to cover the record player as well.

Break the Bank

The cab sped them from Grand Central Station to the Hotel St. George for a brief stay before sailing. Their hotel was located in the heart of scenic Brooklyn Heights, only one subway stop away from Manhattan. Although the room was quite comfortable, they had no idea that they were guests at a New York landmark and that it had once been the largest hotel in the whole city. It was actually a collection of buildings that occupied an entire block, the largest being the thirty-story St. George Tower. The subway station was in the hotel itself, right before the main door leading to one of many ballrooms and the reception desk. The hotel not only boasted the largest banquet room in the world, but also the largest indoor salt-water pool in the United States, with a floor-to-ceiling waterfall at the shallow end that could be seen from several levels.

The Bedfords were fortunate enough to have two sets of knowledgeable guides to help them make the most of their time in New York. The first consisted of none other than the directors of the Spanish Language Institute, who were there on furlough. Mrs. La Porte had transformed from Ben's bête noire into a charming hostess. They took them on the ferry to the Statue of Liberty and even accompanied them to "Break the Bank" at the ABC studio one morning.

Before each broadcast fifteen couples were selected from the studio audience, only four or five of which actually got on the air. Host Bud Collyer made the initial selection by pointing out his choices to staff members stationed in the audience with microphones. The goal was to answer a series of questions and get eight correct answers before making two mistakes. Each correct answer was worth progressively more: $25, $50, $100, $200, $300, $400, $500 and, finally, whatever was in the "bank." The last question was worth the pool of all previous incorrect answers, starting at $1000. On stage, contestants chose from several categories of questions, prepared by Joseph Nathan Kane, author of *Famous First Facts*, and hand delivered to the studio in sealed envelopes.

To their amazement, Bud Collyer picked Ben and La Nell from the audience and they found themselves on stage while Mrs. La Porte looked after David. They chose "Famous Davids" and answered seven questions correctly, with only one error, before reaching the final question to "break the bank." Though they racked their brains, they were unable to come up with "David Glasgow Farragay" in time as the Civil War naval commander in the Battle of New Orleans.

Bud Collyer was charming to them and asked La Nell if she had a perm. "Yes," she replied, "it's a Toni." Delighted, Collyer bowed to her repeatedly saying, "Thank you, thank you!" for Toni was one of the show's sponsors, and when he espied David, he said, "Keep going—you sure did well the first time!"

So Ben and La Nell left the studio five hundred dollars richer, much to the delight of La Wanna and the huge audience of friends and relatives she had drummed up in New Mexico. They were able to replace David's stolen record player and have something in hand to help them set up house again. The La Portes treated them to a celebratory lunch downtown.

Their other guide in New York was a long-time resident, brother to one of the church members from Ranchvale. One night he took them out for dinner, a walk downtown and a thrilling view from the top of the Empire State Building. While they were strolling around Manhattan they stopped to look at a lavish display in a bookstore window. There stood an enormous open book, and every few seconds a page turned automatically. "See, Daddy!" exclaimed David, "I knew a book could turn its own pages!"

Wedding day of Ben's parents, Benjamin Franklin Bedford and Nancy
Tennessee Anthony, Indian Territory (Oklahoma), 1900

La Nell's father, John Watson, Texas, ca. 1910

Ben (right) and brother Ira (left), wearing blue felt hats, Clovis, New Mexico, 1932

La Nell during high school, Bethel, New Mexico, 1942

Church building and parsonage of the first church pastored by Ben,
Pleasant Hill, New Mexico, 1943

Ben's mentor Dr. Aulick with his wife, Portales, New Mexico, ca. 1945

La Nell and Ben's wedding, First Baptist Church, Portales, New Mexico, 1946

La Nell and Ben in front of their garage apartment shortly after their honeymoon, Portales, New Mexico, 1946

La Nell and Ben in front of the parsonage, Ranchvale, New Mexico, 1947

La Nell, Ben and David on the way to Costa Rica, Clovis Air Force Base,
Clovis, New Mexico, 1951

La Nell in traditional Costa Rican dress, San José, Costa Rica, 1952

La Nell, Ben and David boarding the ship for Argentina, New York, 1953

David on the sidewalk in front of the apartment on Avenida Pelligrini,
Rosario, Argentina, 1953

William Ferrell, David, Ben and Nelda in Parque Independencia, Rosario, Argentina, 1954

David in traditional Argentine *gaucho* dress and Nelda in cowgirl attire, Fort Worth, Texas, 1956

Nelda Bedford Gaydou

Front of the First Baptist Church from the inauguration program, Rosario, Argentina, 1958

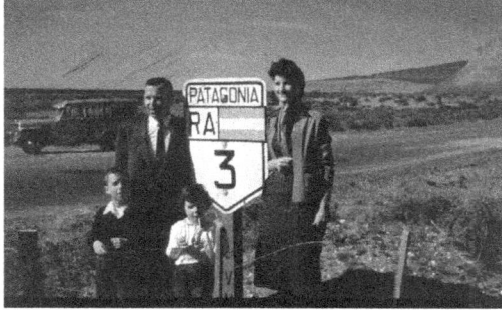

Bedfords on reconnaissance trip to Comodoro Rivadavia, Argentine Patagonia, 1958

Nelda in front of the house on Urquiza, ready for first grade and wearing a *guardapolvo*, Comodoro Rivadavia, Argentina, 1960

Nelda, David and a friend admiring the view of the city and the Atlantic
Ocean from the Chenque, Comodoro Rivadavia, Argentina, 1961

Clockwise, from top left, La Nell, her mother Nora, Nelda and Nancy, sitting
on the steps of Mrs. Watson's house, Portales, New Mexico, 1963

Southbound

Although it was geographical nonsense to go so far north to sail south, leaving from New York made perfect financial sense because the Moore-MacCormack shipping line offered the Foreign Mission Board by far the best rates. The leisurely three-week voyage gave their missionaries time to relax and pull themselves together before being plunged into their new lives.

The Bedfords had a corner stateroom with two portholes. They slept well and ate well, and had a great time swimming and playing games. They met all sorts of people from many parts of the world, including missionaries of several denominations who went along disembarking at different ports along the way. The question they got asked most frequently was, "Where did you go to Bible school?" The ship even had a chapel where services were held, and Ben was asked to speak twice. They got their first glimpse of the Southern Cross from the deck one starry night and received certificates commemorating their first time to cross the Equator.

The ship sailed from spring into fall and made a couple of stops in Brazil. The Bedfords were shown around Rio de Janeiro and its famous Cristo Redentor—the largest Art Deco statue in the world— that looks out over one of the most spectacular views on earth. Their guide was Miss Ray Buster, one of the first foreign missionaries to come out of Ben's childhood church in Clovis, New Mexico. They were delighted to discover that their language school Spanish allowed them to understand and communicate the basics to the Portuguese-speaking Brazilians.

The voyage also gave the Bedfords time to think and pray about their upcoming assignment in Argentina. They had been asked to consider two possible destinations: Buenos Aires and northern Santa Fe Province. When they reached the capital of

Uruguay, Montevideo, Argentine immigration officers got on board to speed along the paperwork while the ship made its way to Buenos Aires across the Río de La Plata, the widest river in the world. The officers gravely went through every scrap of paper, stamping vigorously as they went, and then returned the passports to their owners, that is, until they reached the Bedfords, when they shook their heads grimly, and, instead of returning their documents, gave them a slip of paper to be presented in Buenos Aires.

In Buenos Aires they discovered that the long delay in getting their visas had resulted in two official faux pas. The first, though annoying, was simple. It seemed rather unfair to be upbraided for something the Argentine consul had done on his own initiative, namely, to exempt them from the administrative fee based on Ben's status as a minister. It was now made clear to them that this applied only to Catholic ministers. The fee had to be paid either at the Consulate or downtown at the office of the Ministry of Foreign Relations before they could get their passports back.

The second matter had more serious ramifications. It transpired that the regulations on which goods could be brought in from abroad had changed since the last missionaries had entered the country. Only one new domestic appliance was now allowed, and they had brought three. They would have to choose one for now and leave the other two at the "Aduana" or Customs House, to be negotiated for later on. They chose the refrigerator and watched glumly as the official slid their file into the huge wall of paper behind him.

They were met by the Watsons (no relation) and by Judson Blair, the Mission Secretary, who gave them another jolt by asking, "Should we just have your things sent directly to Rosario?" The Watsons had moved from that city to Buenos Aires along with the Bible Institute when it merged with the International Seminary. Now a missionary was needed for the Greater Rosario Area and the Mission had decided to send the Bedfords. They would be going in two to three weeks. Meanwhile, they were dropped off at a hotel downtown, from which they could see the Presidential Palace, the "Casa Rosada."[26]

---

[26] Pink House

So far they had seen the urban sprawl of Los Angeles, the neoclassic simplicity of Washington, D.C., the towering skyscrapers of New York and the imposing setting of Rio de Janeiro, but Buenos Aires was something altogether different. At that time it was the second largest city in Latin America and the fifth largest in the world. The greater metropolitan area held fully one third of the nation's entire population.

Buenos Aires, beautiful and sophisticated, was known as the Queen of the Plata and the Paris of Latin America. Although it was founded in the fifteen hundreds, most of its buildings dated from the renovations and growth of the late nineteenth and early twentieth centuries. It had both the widest and the longest streets in the world—9 de Julio and Rivadavia. There were broad, tree-lined avenues and inviting parks, statues and fountains, as well as flower-laden wrought-iron balconies. There were shades of Madrid, Barcelona, Rome, Paris and London. Neoclassical, French Renaissance, Art Deco, Art Nouveau, New Gothic and Colonial architecture blended together to reflect the fascinating melting pot that the city had become.

Buses, trains and subways abounded. Although cars and buses had been driving on the right since June of 1945, trains and subways continued to run on the left as they had been doing since they were built by the British (and still do, to the confusion of the logically minded who are unaware of the reason behind it). Unfortunately, the Bedfords were unable to do much sightseeing because they arrived in the middle of a polio epidemic and children were not to be taken to crowded public places.

The Watsons invited them to stay at their house so they wouldn't feel so isolated. Jim took Ben to Rosario to show him the ropes and La Nell offered to take care of the three Watson boys so that Frances could catch a few days of rest in Mendoza. While La Nell was wowing the boys with her cooking in Buenos Aires, Ben was being swept through a dizzying array of introductions up in Rosario. On his first Sunday in the country, he preached at two different churches—Distrito Sud and Barrio Belgrano. He even made a quick trip across the Paraná River by ferry to the capital of the Entre Ríos Province, which bears the same name as that legendary body of water.

When they had all regrouped, the Bedfords spent their last few days in Buenos Aires in a little apartment by the Seminary, from which they made several more trips to the Aduana and acquired a profoundly and genuinely Argentine aversion to bureaucracy.

Chicago on the Pampa

The Bedfords fell in love with Rosario during the ride from the train station down Boulevard Oroño, which, together with Avenida Pellegrini and the Paraná River, formed the unofficial boundary of the downtown district. Majestic palm trees marched down the middle of the broad boulevard throughout its entire length, except where it crossed the landmark Parque Independencia.[27]

They had arrived on the afternoon train, the Rosarino (the morning one being the Porteño[28] in honor of the nation's Capital), covering mile after mile of some of the richest farmland on earth, in places with more than one thousand feet of topsoil, and seeing hundreds upon hundreds of cows grazing on the lush Pampa grasses. When the taxi driver saw their mound of suitcases and trunks, he shook his head: "They will never fit in a taxi." He laughed at the dismay on their faces and swept his arm toward a horse-drawn cart parked nearby. It was soon piled high with their luggage and followed them to their destination.

Unlike other major Argentine cities, Rosario, at that time the second largest in the nation with over six hundred thousand inhabitants, had no glorious colonial heritage. It had begun as a humble little collection of houses near the river in the late eighteenth century. It did not gain city status until 1851, after supporting victorious "*caudillo*"[29] Justo José de Urquiza's bid for national

---

[27] Independence Park
[28] "*Porteño*" means "from Buenos Aires," derived from the Spanish word for "port"
[29] Strongman

power. By 1890 it had become an export outlet and its population had swelled to about fifty thousand, approximately forty percent of which consisted of politically progressive European immigrants. There were three separate attempts to make it the capital of the nation, vetoed each time by the Executive Branch (once by Mitre and twice by Sarmiento). By 1926 there were close to half a million inhabitants, forty-three percent of whom were Europeans who had flocked to the New World in the aftermath of World War I. In 1946 the city massively supported the rise to power of Juan Domingo Perón, who returned the favor with large industrial subsidies. Because of its industries and its standing as a major freshwater grain and cattle port, Rosario was nicknamed the "Chicago" of Argentina.

For the first few days the Bedfords stayed at the apartment of Helen Nixon, a single missionary who was temporarily substituting for Irene Smith as director of a good will center in Buenos Aires. The very first thing they unpacked was David's little red tricycle, which they had dismantled and placed in one of their trunks for easy access. As soon as it was reassembled David joyfully sped down the hallway, where he got stuck in a corner. As he struggled, La Nell admonished him, "Use your head, David."

"My head??" answered the clearly puzzled little boy.

The next day he sounded as if he had a cold coming on and his mother commented, "You sound like you're a little hoarse."

David looked at her reproachfully, unwilling to be caught out again: "A 'horse,' Mommy?!"

The Mission had rented a house first for the Hawkins and then for the Watsons, who had just moved to Buenos Aires, and there were still three years left on the lease, so the Bedfords were expected to live there. When they went to see it, they were aghast. It was enormous, with a huge office, dining room and kitchen downstairs, and four bedrooms upstairs, to say nothing of the maid's quarters. All of their earthly possessions would not have filled even one of the rooms. The thing was clearly impossible, but the Mission was adamant because of the contract.

Ben had already been called to pastor the Distrito Sud church and he confided the problem with their proposed living arrangements to Alberto Pizzicatti, chairman of the deacons.

Pizzicatti, who held a doctorate in economics and was the general manager of Rosario's electric power company, was a born problem solver. He suggested finding someone to sublet the house and renting a smaller place for themselves. The Mission cautiously agreed to the plan, as long as it didn't cost anything extra.

Accordingly, Ben spoke to the owners and told them he would find someone to sublet the house, but they agreed to terminate the contract with no penalties, preferring to choose the new tenant themselves. Ben found a nice little two-bedroom apartment on Avenida Pellegrini that occupied the front half of the ground floor. Another tenant lived in the apartment at the back, while the owner occupied the entire second floor. There was even enough money left over to rent an office downtown.

By the time they moved into their new home, the Bedfords had already been officially welcomed to their new church, and interviewed and written up in *El Heraldo Bautista*,[30] the local Association's news magazine, complete with a summary of their lives and ministry, as well as two photographs—one of Ben, La Nell and David, and the other of Ben with a group of pastors and leaders from Rosario. The writers professed themselves to be thrilled at finally having a real, live Texan in their midst and reported that they realized it was time to end the interview when they saw David targeting them with a toy gun converted into a rifle by the simple expedient of adding a stick to the barrel.

When the Bedfords' shipment, minus washing machine and stove, was released from Customs, they had a refrigerator, David's basic bedroom furniture and his parents' mattress and box springs with which to furnish their apartment. Pizziccatti came to the rescue again, recommending a furniture maker from one of the local churches, who made and financed a truly beautiful living- and dining-room set of blond wood and leather for them.

For transportation, they inherited a huge black Humber from the early thirties that took them back at a glance to the days when Churchill had become famous. It had once been a magnificent vehicle meant to be driven by a chauffeur and was equipped with a glass partition to separate him from his passengers. And, of course, the steering wheel was on the right. The Hawkins had needed the

---

[30] The Baptist Herald

space in the back—two rows of fixed seats plus two auxiliary ones that folded at the sides—to drive their band around. But now the poor thing was more than a little arthritic and it was advisable to park it on an incline with clear space ahead to ensure ignition. The young people at the church became quite used to pushing when it wouldn't start rolling on its own. Fortunately, there were several alternative modes of transportation. Bicycles were very popular in Rosario and, in fact, the entire Santa Fe Province. The Bedfords were soon equipped with their own and used them or the trolley most of the time to get around town.

Kinning

When they first heard the term "kinning" twenty-five years later, the Bedfords realized that their experience in Rosario was a textbook example of forming kinships to adapt to a new culture. To the fellowship that the Christian church offers all believers, the congregation at Distrito Sud added all of the Argentine warmth and affection. They adopted the Bedfords as their own and showered them with love. They discovered exactly what Jesus meant when he said, "And everyone who has left houses or brothers or sisters or father or mother or children or fields for my sake will receive a hundred times as much."[31] The bonds forged at Distrito Sud were to be among the strongest and most long-lasting of their lives.

Julio and Pilar Loredo lived perhaps five blocks away from the church. They had two sons, Ignacio and Julio, and a daughter, Esther. Don Julio was an accountant and served as the church's secretary, while Pilar taught small children in Sunday School, including David. The Loredos treated Ben and La Nell as if they were their own children. They had an impressive collection of birds and gave David a beautiful canary named after the famous tenor Eddie Cantor. A female was soon added to keep him company. David saw them mating and was concerned.

"Mommy, why is Eddie so mean to Molly?" he wanted to know.

La Nell explained that he wasn't being mean, that he was just doing what birds must do to have babies. He thought that over and wanted to know if other animals had to do the same thing. When he got an affirmative answer, his eyes grew huge as he struggled with the concept.

---

[31] Matthew 19:29

"Then, how does a bull do it?!!"

Don Julio personified the contradictory Argentine traits of brutal honesty and fear of hurting someone's feelings. On one occasion he and Ben visited a man who was eager to try out his English. It was truly atrocious, but Ben gallantly told him that his English was probably better than his Spanish. Once they were on the sidewalk after their farewells, Don Julio was reproachful—"I think you might have hurt his feelings!"—which left Ben wondering exactly how poor he considered his language skills.

The Vicentes, all of whose children were grown, except for Nelly, became David's newest set of self-appointed grandparents. They loved to take him home for lunch after the Sunday morning worship service and soon established a priority claim on his company, whether or not his parents could be there. Ben took Don Manuel on rounds with him many times.

José Simari, a widower who lived next door to the church building, owned and operated a small factory that made caramel candies year round and ice-cream waffle cones in the summer with the help of his daughter Porota and four sons Cacho, Rubén, Pepe and Abel, employing people from the church whenever he could. He was a powerful and effective lay preacher.

He was also another of Ben's frequent visitation partners. One day they had had a positive marathon of about ten visits in a row, and they were hospitably offered some sort of refreshment at each place. The last visit was to the Martíns' stand at the market. Of course Mr. Martín wanted to give them something to eat and they pleaded that they had already had far too much.

"You'll at least have some orange juice!" he exclaimed. Actually, freshly squeezed orange juice sounded great, and they accepted. Ben noticed something unusual in the flavor and it rather burned going down.

"You know," he said as they headed home, "if I didn't know any better, I'd say that orange juice had been spiked with something."

"Huh," replied Don Simari. "That was practically pure whisky!"

The first Christmas that the Bedfords were there, they had a houseful of missionaries with them—the Garners, the Ferrells, the Freemans and Chris Eidson—and they visited their church on Sunday, but their guests, all from the Southern U.S. teetotaler culture, did not partake of the Lord's Supper because real wine was served. Don Simari was concerned when he noticed their empty hands and, in a stage whisper heard by every person in the congregation, asked Ben to let them know they were welcome to participate. Ben whispered back not to worry and that he would explain later. Ben had learned to simply go with the flow on this issue, although later on, in a church which had communion every Sunday and used a very strong wine that required him to make a great effort to keep his lips from puckering, he did implore the congregation, "If you are going to use wine, at least use a good one!"

There were five deacons when the Bedfords arrived: Alberto Pizzicatti, his sister Irma, Julio Loredo, José Simari and Floduardo Farías. Alberto was the chairman and had been a strong and positive role model for the entire church. They had been without a pastor for five years and the laymen had done an exceptional job of keeping things going. The deacons were used to turning their hands to whatever needed to be done, but had been willing to give others in the congregation opportunities to participate and serve, including the young people. They were ready to go the next level and game for anything. Ben had only to make a suggestion—"How do you feel about...?"—for them to take it up, embellish it and put it into practice.

It was a gifted group, with people ready and willing to speak, lead and sing. They came from all walks of life: bookkeepers, lawyers, teachers, butchers, grocers, construction workers, carpenters, masons and candy-makers. Surnames were Spanish, Italian, German, French, Ukrainian, Yugoslav and British, but mostly Italian. In addition to the *chau*[32] with which Argentines take their leave, Ben picked up Italian expressions that stayed with him forever, notably *eccolo qua*, usually shortened to *ecco*, literally "here it is" but often use as a confirmatory "that's it." He also discovered that the soft *boina* or beret so beloved of Italians and Spaniards was just the thing to protect his head against the winter cold.

Rosario was home to two professional soccer teams and the population was pretty much split down the middle in a Yankees-Dodgers type of rivalry that transcended social class, ethnic origin and religion. Baptists were no exception to this rule so Sundays were very full days for some church members. After Sunday School

[32] Spanish spelling of the Italian "ciao"

and the morning worship service, devoted fans would head for the stadiums to support either Rosario Central (blue and yellow) or Newells Old Boys (red and black), making it back just in time for Training Union and the evening service.

Although they were rapidly assimilating the language and the culture, the Bedfords couldn't help but provide their new congregation with some unintentional amusement. In preparation for a High Attendance Day in Sunday School, church members made a huge paper chain, printing a name on each link. On the Sunday before the special event, Ben exhorted the members not to miss it: "*¡No sea usted el que rompa la cadena del servicio!*"[33] People started giggling and snorting with laughter. Ben's Spanish had actually been flawless, but unfortunately the phrase lent itself to an embarrassing double entendre: "service" meant both "service" and "water closet," and the toilet in the church building was of an old-fashioned pull-chain model, which with unwittingly impeccable timing could be heard flushing faintly in the background.

---

[33] "Don't be the one to break the service chain!"

The Dating Game

Courtships in Argentina were quite different from what Ben and La Nell had grown up with, but they quickly learned all about it with the large group of young people at their church. Instead of dating, the standard procedure for a prospective couple was to spend a long time talking and getting to know each other within the safe confines of their social group until they were sure enough to make a commitment.

Rubén Simari gave every sign of being very interested in Sarita, the eldest of the Ávalos girls. Anita was really too young for the group but their mother, Doña Magdalena, wouldn't hear of Sarita going alone, and usually chaperoned the proceedings from a back seat. Once in a while she would agree to leave the girls with the group, as long as it was understood that they would be walked home. Of course, Rubén always made sure he was in the accompanying party.

The first of the Simari siblings, Porota, had married and lived in nearby Pérez. Rubén would often visit her on Sunday after the evening service. The Baptist world being tightly knit, word soon got around that Rubén was lavishing rather a lot of attention on a cute girl in the Pérez congregation. Ben brought to bear all of his weight as pastor and friend to let Rubén know in no uncertain terms that he had to curb his Don Juanesque tendencies and refrain from leading on two girls at the same time. He needed to decide on one or the other. Rubén was often to reminisce, while shaking a hand eloquently, "*¡El pastor Bedford me enderezó!*"[34] Rubén searched his heart and devoted himself thereafter to Sarita. He married her several years later on the Bedford's wedding anniversary.

---

[34] "Pastor Bedford straightened me out!"

One of Ben and La Nell's favorites among the young women was Sonia Schneider, who lived up the street with her grandfather and two cousins, her widowed father having remarried and relocated to the mountains of Córdoba where he ran a charming inn. They were rather hoping that Sonia and Ignacio Loredo would hit it off, but he chose María Teresa from the Women's Institute before it was incorporated into the new Seminary in Buenos Aires. Some time later, when she was studying at the Seminary, Sonia met and married a fine young man. Meanwhile, her cousin Mabel married Ignacio's brother Julio, of the golden tenor voice. Ben performed both of the brothers' weddings. Their sister Esther was later to marry a pastor, but at this time she was still very young. She belonged to the local female version of the Three Musketeers: Esthercita Loredo, Anita Ávalos and Nelly Vicente. Ben baptized all three of them when they were eleven years old—the youngest people baptized at Distrito Sud up to that time.

While in the U.S. legal marriages could be performed by either justices of the peace or ordained ministers, in Argentina they were performed by the local registrars of the *Registro Nacional de las Personas.*[35] Originally marriages could only be performed by the Roman Catholic Church, excluding persons of other denominations or religions. A national law was enacted to secularize the proceedings after a spirited legal battle in which Baptists played a prominent role. The traditional church ceremonies became dedications and blessings.

Ben did not perform all of the marriage ceremonies for his flock. When Rubén's brother Cacho married Azucena (another catch from the Women's Institute), he asked his longtime mentor and spiritual father Alberto Pizzicatti to do the honors. Another set of brothers who became very close to the Bedfords were Ananías and Azarías González. Ananías was doing his military service when they first arrived and often came to church in his uniform. He worked in Ben's office for a time (followed by Julio and María Teresa). When Ananías married Nelly from the First Baptist Church, the ceremony was performed by her pastor, Floreal Ureta. Alberto Cáceres was already married to a big-hearted nurse named Rosa. His brother Julio was later to become very active in the church as well.

---

[35] Bureau of Vital Statistics

The church recognized the outstanding qualities of its young people, and elected Alberto, Ignacio, Ananías and young Vicente Gianonne as deacons to combine their enthusiasm and fresh ideas with the steadiness and clear-sightedness of the proven older generation.

Slightly Cockeyed

"And please send me a baby sister. Amen," prayed three-year-old David kneeling by his bed in his pajamas. He had been making this particular request for months now. Sure enough, they had barely settled in when La Nell discovered that she was pregnant. Soon she began experiencing RH factor-induced problems. If she was up and about for any length of time she began hemorrhaging, so she was forced to stay home most of the time and spend a great deal of it in bed for the first six months. During that time she learned to knit and translated reams of educational material. But she needed full-time help to care for David and do the housework.

The Baptist community stepped up once again. Pastor Caramutti recommended the daughter of one of his church members. This was sixteen-year-old Lucía, who was so nervous at her interview that she was literally wringing her hands, a phenomenon the Bedfords had only seen in print until that moment. She shyly but proudly informed them that she had completed primary school, which was as far as people who weren't pursuing a profession usually got.

Lucía was a great help in many ways. She saved La Nell countless steps by taking care of most of the domestic chores. She saw to the milkman and the greengrocer who delivered their goods door to door from horse-drawn carts. The milkman ladled milk out of tall cans and Lucía learned to use the gallon-sized home pasteurizer the Bedfords had brought from the States. The greengrocer took advantage of his frequent visits to get to know Lucía, to such good effect that they married several years later. But Lucía did not know how to cook. Neither did Ben, but he taught her. They developed a system that worked beautifully: La Nell explained the preparation of a given dish to Ben; he passed the explanation on to Lucía; and she put it into practice.

Although Lucía adored David, Ben often took his little son with him so she could do the housework unhindered. On Sunday David would behave beautifully throughout the services. His favorite spot was a seat on the second pew on the left. If anyone unwittingly occupied his place, he would just stand in the aisle, staring silently. The unfailing reaction of the unintentional usurper was to scoot over hastily with a sincere but amused, "¡Perdoname!"[36]

Since La Nell could not travel, Ben went to his very first Mission Meeting alone three months after arriving in Argentina. It was held at the still unfinished new Seminary building in Buenos Aires and by the end of it he had been voted President of the Río de La Plata Mission for an eventful year—the fiftieth anniversary of the Southern Baptist work in Argentina and the last year before the Argentine and Uruguayan Missions became independent organizations (the Paraguayan Mission had already done so but the three national Conventions were still united).

Although he protested his unsuitability as a new arrival with practically no knowledge of how things were done, the missionaries were adamant that he should accept. They had divided like the Red Sea into two opposing factions and he was the only neutral person there. Times were changing and, although everyone meant well, there were apparently irreconcilable differences between them. The older generation clung to an old benevolent paternalism toward the nationals while the younger generation saw the need to promote and empower local leadership.

So Ben was thrust into the role of peacemaker between the missionaries and represented the Mission at the numerous anniversary celebrations all over the country, where he met many of the Argentine leaders. He also visited fields from which missionaries were about to retire to get a sense of their needs and make informed recommendations.

One of these trips was to southwest Argentina, which the Bowdlers would soon be leaving. Bowdler met Ben's train in General Roca and drove him around the area in his old De Soto. He left Ben in Cippoletti, heart of the apple-growing country, in the care

---

[36] Forgive me! [The lack of accent in the Spanish "perdoname" is not a typographical error for Argentines, like many other Latin Americans, use the voseo rather than the tuteo form for the informal "you."]

of Daniel Gaydou, a young pastor who had been a bone of contention between Bowdler and Swenson. The latter worked in the southeast area and felt that Bowdler had "stolen" Gaydou from his pastorate in Punta Alta. Daniel and his wife Dolores (affectionately known as "Lola") had two small boys at that time, Daniel and Alberto. Little did Ben know that the first would one day be his student at the Seminary and the second would become his son-in-law.

Rosario offered a broad network of public transportation. Although the Humber was finally traded in for a piece of property and the Bedfords fell heir to the Robertsons' 1937 Ford when they went on furlough, neither vehicle was up to much of a drive, and Ben rode his bicycle or public transportation most of the time. At his first physical exam on the field, the doctor sternly warned him to give up smoking. To his indignant protest that he had never smoked the doctor opposed his chest x-ray, which looked like that of a life-time heavy smoker, all from second-hand smoke in the trains and buses.

The Bedfords were not the only missionaries in Rosario. Besides Helen Nixon, whose apartment they had lived in for the first few weeks, they were soon joined by Billy and Ada Graves, with their daughter Sally Kate. They shared a special love for Christian Education and soon the two couples became close friends who enjoyed working and playing together. Another single missionary lady in their city was Sarah Taylor, who directed the *Casa de Amistad*,[37] offering kindergarten and numerous other social services to the Rosario Baptists and the community in general. They were struck right away with her language skills when she handled an elderly Italian man with no apparent difficulty.

"What did he say?" asked Ben. "I didn't understand a single word of it!"

"Neither did I," replied Sarah matter-of-factly. "I just smile and nod my head and make sympathetic noises."

One day Sarah informed La Nell that David had told her that his mommy said she was "a little cockeyed." Blushing, La Nell was forced to recount a recent conversation with her little son, who had overheard the grownups talking and saying something was "cockeyed."

---

[37] Good Will Center

"What does 'cockeyed' mean, Mommy?"

"It just means that something is not quite right, like when someone's eyes are slightly crossed or crooked."

"Like Sarah T?"

"Well, I guess you could say that she is a little cockeyed."

A Sister for David

David was a hard act for any child to follow. It was difficult to imagine how anyone could compete with his bright brown eyes, sunny disposition and precocious vocabulary. He charmed everyone. Fortunately for the next Bedford, widespread approval was guaranteed because the child would be a genuine Argentine.

Except for the fact that both babies were born in the summer, although the first child was born in July and the second in January, the two experiences were very different. When she had David, La Nell had been knocked out with anesthesia. On the positive side, she had skipped quite a bit of the pain, but she had had to wait over twelve hours to see her newborn because the staff was too busy to bother with them. This time around the staff was all loving attention but the process was completely natural, totally unassisted by any kind of painkiller. La Nell was therefore very aware when her 3.4 kilogram[38] baby made it out into the world and the doctor presented her with her tiny daughter teasing, "She's perfect, except for lacking a little bit of nose."

The baby was placed in her mother's room, but La Nell's pleasure in the arrangement was somewhat dampened by the newborn's insistent bawling. She called the nurse and asked her what she thought the problem might be.

"She's cold," diagnosed the nurse and proceeded to double a blanket over twice and tuck it around the baby.

"Cold!" exclaimed La Nell. It had to be the hottest day of the year, very humid and unrelieved by air-conditioning. Sweat was pouring down the poor nurse and everyone else in the hospital. But,

---

[38] 7.5 lb

sure enough, the little one relaxed and fell into a blissfully silent sleep.

The new baby had dual citizenship: U.S. because of her parents and Argentine due to her place of birth. Of course that meant double the red tape. Ben had to fill out a record of birth at the U.S. Consulate in Buenos Aires for little Nelda Anne. Locally, she had to be registered at the Rosario office of the *Registro Nacional de las Personas*.[39] Here he hit an unexpected snag—the first name was not on the official list. In an effort to promote some semblance of linguistic harmony among the multitude of languages brought in by the immigrants, the government had decreed an approved list, consisting of names of Spanish origin, names of saints and other traditional names. It included "Nilda" and "Nélida," but not "Nelda." The clerk filling out the form took pity on Ben's plight.

"I'll tell you what: we'll register her as 'Nilda' but I will make a 'mistake' as I write it down and once it is written as 'Nelda,' it will stand." The little girl thus officially became "Nelda Ana Bedford."

Apart from the shock La Nell got when David appeared at the hospital with a bandage covering a gash on the back of his head, the result of a knock from being too much underfoot when his father climbed down from retrieving the camera that had been on top of a tall piece of furniture, it was all plain sailing. Nelda was a normal, healthy baby. Their Argentine friends were enchanted and considered that they now had the perfect family with their *parejita*[40] of children, a boy and a girl, with just the right contrast: blond hair and brown eyes for him, brown hair and blue eyes for her. David was delighted and very protective. The only damper was everyone's constant raving over his little sister being a Rosarina, which finally prompted him to ask, "When will *I* be a Rosarino, Mommy?" La Nell did her best to convince him that nothing could be better than being a Texan.

---

[39] Bureau of Vital Statistics
[40] Little couple

What Daddy Did

La Nell unwittingly revolutionized the Baptist world. She quickly regained her strength after having the baby and eagerly plunged into all sorts of activities. There was an associational volleyball league for men and another for women, and Ben and La Nell joined the respective teams from their church. The revolution took place when La Nell appeared in shorts, a first in the very conservative Baptist circle. It was an immediate success and the new fashion spread like wildfire.

She also impressed the young people with her ping-pong prowess. Special meetings were often held after the Sunday evening service. While Ben was cooped up with the deacons or some committee or other, La Nell would head over to the Young People's Annex and give them a good workout with the skills she had acquired over a long and distinguished career in table-tennis at church and college. There was always someone willing to hold and entertain the baby.

The Bedfords found that having small children made it easy to talk to everyone, because Argentines of all ages and social positions absolutely loved them. On one memorable family outing, the train developed some sort of mechanical problem that made the whole thing jump every time the wheel went around, and this went on for a very long time. All things being equal, everyone would have been annoyed and complaining, but Nelda, who was just a few months old, giggled hilariously every time it happened and kept the whole carriage entertained and laughing with her.

Small children were usually cared for during the church services so their parents could get the full benefit of the sermons, for which La Nell was usually very grateful. She was not so grateful—in fact, she was thoroughly incensed—when Nelda caught the whooping cough at the nursery. The indignation stemmed from the fact that the sick child had been taken there by her grandmother, who was a nurse and should have known better.

Sometimes child care was not available and La Nell had to keep the little one as entertained and quiet as possible, at times by the simple expedient of stuffing a cracker in her mouth (something that had to be done very quickly once Nelda started saying "cracker" since her early attempts sounded a lot like "ca-ca," which meant something altogether different in Spanish[41]). If things got out of hand, La Nell would take the little girl out to remonstrate with her. She was usually waylaid by someone who would say, "*No le pegue, señora; ¡yo se la tengo!*"[42] But La Nell had an irrefutable argument: "*¿Ven lo bien que se porta David? ¿Cómo creen que sucedió eso?*"[43]

Nelda was a special pet of some of the young people, who loved to tease her about her thumb-sucking. One day she let them go on and on about it for a good long while. Then, with impeccable timing, she looked them in the eye and slowly lowered her hand, showing them that her thumb had been tucked into her fist the whole time. Fortunately, they were even more delighted with her for having hoodwinked them. But one Sunday night she broke up the entire service. It was a special meeting and this would be her first time to see a baptism, since up to now she had always been in the nursery. She was getting restless and fidgety, but La Nell did not want to miss it, so she whispered, "*Mirá; ¡mirá lo que va a hacer tu papá!*"[44] Nelda watched obediently, holding her breath, and at the most beautiful and solemn moment when Ben lowered the new Christian into the water and raised him back up, she gasped out, "*Ay, ¡lo que hizo mi papá!*"[45] It took several minutes for everyone to regain their composure and dry their tears...of laughter.

---

[41] Pooh

[42] "Don't spank her; I'll hold her for you!"

[43] "See how well David behaves? How do you think that happened?"

[44] "Look; see what your Daddy is going to do!"

[45] "Oooh, what my Daddy did!"

The Ripple Effect

Somehow, the idea of a Sunday School enlargement campaign at the Distrito Sud church mushroomed into a citywide effort with guest participants from all over the country, missionaries from every area and even guest speakers from abroad. Sunday School preparation and attendance shot up everywhere and the campaign developed the unexpected offshoot of a long series of important building projects. And the Bedfords were in the thick of it all.

In their interview for the Baptist news magazine *El Heraldo Bautista*,[46] they had been asked for their impression of Rosario.

> *"Oh, the people here are very kind! We feel that this is where the Lord wants us to dedicate our lives to his Cause."*

> *"What do you think of your church?" We were referring to the Distrito Sud church, of which he is the brand-new pastor.*

> *"I like the brothers. Especially seeing how well they perform the church tasks. I see many opportunities for the Work in this church. And that is why I have accepted being their pastor, because I know that when my obligations as a missionary require my absence, there will be responsible and capable people to trust."*

> *"So your work in the church won't tie you down and you will dedicate part of your time to the general work?"*

> *"That's right, he answered. At this time I'm working on a personal work plan. When it is ready I will share it with all of the churches to put myself at their service during the time I can set aside for that purpose."*

---

[46] The Baptist Herald

So Ben had plunged into the work at his own church and left its capable leaders in charge some Sunday nights in order to visit the other churches and get to know them and their leaders, sometimes preaching, sometimes simply sharing services as part of the congregation, always participating in long and productive talks, often over a cup of coffee.

Ben and La Nell were well versed in the latest Sunday School materials and teaching methods since New Mexico had been the proving grounds on which they had been tried and tested. They told their church all about the basic idea, which involved placing the congregation into age groups—Nursery, Toddlers, Beginners, Juniors, Intermediates, Young People and Adults—and providing each class with age-appropriate materials and teachers trained to carry out a systematic study of the Bible. The people of Distrito Sud were enthusiastic and readily agreed that it would be good to invite the other churches in the area to take advantage of the training opportunities.

Obviously, it would be ideal to have not only general but also specialized age-specific training. The plan began to take shape. Each church would try to have at least one prospective teacher for each group and the Bedfords would see to finding teachers to do the training—one teacher for each age group for each of the eleven participating churches. Missionaries and experienced national teachers were invited and pressed into service. As a result, churches all over the country became aware of the project and many asked if they could send representatives to participate, learn and take the knowledge back home to set up their own program. Of course they were welcomed.

A week-long program was planned, with general sessions in the mornings at the Good Will Center and hands-on training in the evenings at the individual churches, culminating with a joint service at the First Baptist Church on Sunday night. Arrangements were made to pair hosts and visitors for housing and meals. The potential of the event was tremendous. Ben suggested taking advantage of this gathering of so many teachers and pastors to bring in top qualified speakers gifted in training and communicating a broad vision of Christian education.

The Foreign Mission Board came up trumps for the occasion. They sent Frank W. Patterson, affectionately known as Dr. Pat,

Andrew S. Allen and Jasper Newton "J.N." Barnette, three living legends of Religious Education. Dr. Patterson, the general director of the Spanish Baptist Publishing House in El Paso, or Casa Bautista, was a former missionary with a passion for writing and teaching who was credited with transforming the publishing house from a small print shop into a powerhouse that provided Christian curricula and literature to the entire Spanish-speaking world. Andrew Allen was the Director of Sunday School Activities for the Baptist General Convention of Texas, as well as the President of the Baptist Religious Education Association. He was an important part of many teams that helped expand church religious education programs not only in the United States, but around the world, as far away as Japan. For his part, J.N. Barnette was on the Sunday School Board of the Southern Baptist Convention. He was known as "Mr. Sunday School" and was the father of the "Million More in '54" campaign, whose goal was to enroll one million new students in Sunday School during that year. Although that number was not quite reached, it did drive the Southern Baptists in the U.S. to have the largest Sunday School movement in recorded church history. This growth in Bible study in turn spurred growth in many other areas, including evangelism, training, music, study courses and missions, and was the catalyst for the creation of the in-house Convention Press for denominational curricula in 1955.

The whole thing was a roaring success. Not only did the churches in the Rosario area get a tremendous boost in their Christian Education programs and training, but the visiting pastors and teachers took the vision back to their own churches and fields, and some of the participants were later to become leaders in the religious education and publishing areas of the Argentine Baptist Convention.

J.N. Barnette worked most closely with the group that met at the First Baptist Church and became so interested in it that when he returned to the U.S. he gave a very enthusiastic account of his experience to Maxey Jarman, a Baptist businessman from Tennessee who had made millions in his shoe business and, after touring Latin America, had given large amounts of money to the Foreign Mission Board, earmarked for purchasing properties and constructing attractive church buildings on the main avenues of the principal cities of Latin America. Jarman was so impressed with Barnette's story that he wrote out a check for one hundred thousand

dollars on the spot, to be spent on a building for the First Baptist
Church of Rosario.

Bagfuls of Money

Ben and Bill nonchalantly tucked their respective satchels, each stuffed with ten thousand dollars' worth of Argentine pesos, behind their legs under the seats of the train. Bill Graves had recently arrived to work in religious education in Rosario and had gotten thrown directly into the deep end of the Argentine way of doing business. Ben, with a year's seniority, had already been entered into quite a variety of events.

This particular incident was the result of a currency exchange transaction. The Foreign Mission Board had sent a large number of dollars to Buenos Aires and had come to an agreement with the Remington-Rand company, which had the pesos and needed the dollars. The official rate at that time was fourteen pesos to the dollar, but the government allowed certain entities to make the exchange at twenty-one pesos to the dollar. This smacked of the black market to the FMB and it decided that the Argentine Mission could not accept it without offending the donor. The officer from Remington-Rand countered that he had to make the exchange at the higher rate and was not allowed to keep the difference. After some head-scratching, the Mission decided to take the twenty-thousand peso difference and assign it to the next name on the building project list. That happened to be the Distrito Sud Church in Rosario, so area missionaries Bedford and Graves were chosen as couriers.

Distrito Sud was badly in need of adequate buildings. Its main property, whose adobe walls were forty-five centimeters thick,[47] had originally belonged to a mortuary company and had housed horse-drawn hearses. Shortly after the Bedfords arrived the church had the opportunity of buying the house next door to serve as the

---

[47] Eighteen inches

156

future parsonage. The congregation had the means to make the payments, but the mortgage had to be in the name of an individual, and Ben was asked to lend his name until the loan was paid off.

Several churches began building projects at about the same time, after the Sunday School Enlargement Campaign brought home to them the urgent need for suitable educational facilities in addition to a place for holding worship services. The largest of these was the First Baptist Church, which was able to launch an ambitious building plan thanks to the efforts of its own congregation and the generous Jarman offering. Their current building was on Montevideo Street, but they had purchased an old movie house, the Teatro Ideal, strategically located on San Martín, near Córdoba Avenue, where national Baptist convention meetings had been held. This was to be torn down to make way for the new auditorium, educational building and parsonage.

Pastor Floreal Ureta found the Gut & Ragni firm and took Ben with him to meet the architects. As area missionary, Ben represented the Mission and was considered to be experienced in construction because of a building project back in Ranchvale, New Mexico. The architects had no idea what was needed in a Baptist church, so the two pastors explained the activities that would be carried out there. The concept of the baptistry was particularly novel. Ben had brought along educational materials.

"Those two men who came to the office today are different from anyone I've ever met before," José Ragni told his wife Delia that evening. It was the beginning of a life-long friendship between the Bedfords and the Ragnis. Ben and José soon lost count of the meetings and the hours spent poring over drawings, talking and drinking coffee. José began attending the Sunday night services at the various churches where Ben preached, ostensibly to get a feel for what was needed in the new buildings, but he frequently asked questions regarding the sermons and Ben often gave him reading material. One book José found particularly helpful was a fat tome entitled *The Faith of the New Testament*. He read everything carefully and passed it on to his wife, who in turn devoured it on the hour-long trip between her downtown home and the school on the south side where she taught.

Little did they know that José would eventually prepare plans for over two hundred churches throughout Argentina and become

Chairman of the Convention's Loan Board, and that Delia, who became the state educational supervisor for the entire Santa Fe Province, would one day lead the local and associational Women's Missionary Union, and team up with La Nell to write Sunday School literature, while their daughter Graciela would eventually marry Pastor Ureta's son David. But all of that was yet to come. Meanwhile, José went to Buenos Aires with Ben to study and measure the baptistry in the Seminary's chapel. As they were jotting down notes, Ben said, "Our prayer is that you will be the first one baptized in the new building."

José smiled noncommittally, "Who knows? It's possible." But he continued attending services, often with his wife. Sometimes he even took friends and relatives, always checking first that Ben was preaching. "I like all of the pastors, but I want people to hear the message for the first time from you, because you make it so clear and simple."

The construction projects also created other close ties. Ben spent countless hours with Samuel Elías from the First Baptist Church's Building Committee. He was very knowledgeable, practical and helpful, besides being just plain nice. A strong friendship also grew with the pastor, Floreal Ureta, who probably had one of the best minds in the Baptist world. He was an avid reader and deep thinker, but always retained a very humble spirit. The pastor that preceded him had been there for many years and part of the congregation was never able to imagine anyone else in his place. The church as a whole tended to think that the pastor should be entirely devoted to spiritual matters and often neglected such mundane things as cost-of-living increases. Ureta and his wife, who was born on a ship in the Atlantic while her parents emigrated from Russia to Uruguay, had a large family and lived in barely adequate housing on an amazingly small salary. When Ureta became distant and reserved, Ben knew he was going through an especially rough time and was trying to steel himself to ask for a loan. The Bedfords often helped out with love offerings, and a feeling of mutual respect and friendship grew and prospered over the years.

Although La Nell was not called upon to work in the field in the building projects, she was a key member of the team because she kept all of the books—at one time six different sets at once—while Ben did a lot of legwork and became intimately acquainted with every aspect of the building process, from financing to drawings, obtaining permits, hiring contractors, buying materials and supervising on-site.

Concealed Weapons

Rosario was the natural rest stop for most people traveling to and from Buenos Aires, and the Bedfords therefore often had out-of-town guests for meals and overnight stays in their beautiful little apartment. If there was a couple, Ben and La Nell put them in their bedroom and set up the full-sized roll-away bed for themselves in the garage, while David could share his small room or sleep on bedding set up in the hallway or living room.

The Ferrells arrived a few months after the Bedfords had settled in and stopped by on their way to their new home. In the U.S. Bill, who remained "William" only to his wife Opal, had been heavily involved with the Royal Ambassadors, an organization for school-aged boys, and the Mission had hoped that he would succeed the current RA promoter who was about to retire. Although he never his lost his love for and interest in that work, Bill felt called to field evangelism and accepted the invitation to work as area missionary in Córdoba City, capital of the province with the same name.

David and Curtis were overjoyed at seeing each other again. The families spent their first Christmas in Argentina together and, since the Ferrells stayed with the Bedfords during the Sunday School Enlargement Campaign, they were able to spend every waking moment of that week playing together. The bond became stronger than ever, so it was only natural for Curtis' parents to drop him off in Rosario on their way to their second child's birth in Buenos Aires. The Bedfords were amused at the little boy's clipped affirmatives in the midst of a Mississippi drawl.

"Would you like some of this, Curtis?"

"Yep."

Being *in loco parentis*, Ben would admonish him mildly, "Don't say 'yep,' Curtis."

"Yessir!"

"You don't have to say 'yes, sir.' You can just say 'yes.'"

"Nossir. My daddy told me to say 'yes, sir!'"

When all of the housing and hospital arrangements had been made, Ben took Curtis to Buenos Aires on the train. The ride was fascinating at first, but he was eager to rejoin his parents and see the new baby, so the five-hour trip seemed to stretch out forever.

"Why is it so far from Rosario to Buenos Aires?"

"That's just where the cities were built."

"But, why, Uncle Ben?" he'd ask at increasingly frequent intervals. "Why does it have to take so long?"

In spite of it all, Curtis arrived in time for the birth of his baby sister Lynn.

But what really sealed the friendship of the entire family was the return trip from Mission Meeting. The Bedfords' Humber was out of the question for trips involving more than a few blocks, and the train ride was a bit awkward with a baby and related paraphernalia, so the Ferrells picked them up on the way in their '37 Ford, which was just able to accommodate four adults, two preschoolers and two babies.

On the way back, the car broke down just out of Pergamino, about 100 kilometers[48] from Rosario. Bill was eventually able to hitch a ride into town to find a mechanic. While he was gone, a Good Samaritan took pity on the family party and towed them into town with a rope. They met Bill on the edge of town and found a place to spend the night while the car was being repaired. The unfortunate series of events struck their funny-bone, and the laughter and good spirits set the tone for all of their future dealings.

Nelda was a medium-sized baby with absolutely standard motor skills, but tiny Lynn was something of an acrobat even before she could walk. During one visit La Nell popped in the room to check on the napping babies just in time to catch Lynn by the heel as

---

[48] A little over sixty miles

she climbed out of the crib. In fact, she was always good for a little excitement.

The Bedfords' pediatrician lived just down the street. He had been surprised when he first met them because David did not seem the least bit ill. They explained David's history of harrowing medical experiences and that they didn't want to start off their relationship under unfavorable circumstances that would make the little boy dread him. One day Lynn was playing placidly on the floor and suddenly keeled over, totally unresponsive. La Nell made a frantic call to the doctor who rushed over and was annoyed to see Nelda blithely running around underfoot. "I thought you said the baby needed urgent care!"

"Not that one—this one!"

The doctor took one look, made a quick call, grabbed Lynn up in his arms and, followed closely by Opal, dashed the baby to the hospital, where the staff was waiting with the necessary medication and equipment. By the time the rest of the group got there, the situation was well under control. However, there was no doubt that if it had not been for the neighborhood pediatrician, the little girl would have died that day.

Lynn was not always that dramatic, but she was usually entertaining. On one memorable occasion, much to David and Curtis' delight, while everyone was enjoying a leisurely breakfast, she solemnly picked up her glass of milk and carefully poured it out on the top of her head, from where it ran down in perfect symmetry, like icing on a cake.

Of course it wasn't always the Ferrells visiting the Bedfords. Because it is located along a huge river, Rosario is very humid. Soon the children developed bronchitis and nasty coughs. The doctor recommended mountain air. Alberto Pizzicatti reminded them that Sonia Schneider's father ran a little inn, the Hostería Achalay, in the heart of Córdoba's Punilla Valley. La Nell and the children met Opal, Curtis and Lynn in Córdoba City and stayed together at the Achalay for several days.

It was perfect. The air was wonderful. La Falda, the town in which the inn was located, was considered to have the third healthiest climate in the world (after some place in Israel and another in California). A few miles away there was a famous facility for tuberculosis patients from all over the country. And the setting was extremely picturesque. From the Achalay, perched up on a hill, they could see most of the town down in the valley against a backdrop of mountains, whose two largest peaks in that area were Cerro La Banderita[49] and Cerro El Cuadrado.[50] The town's name means "The Lap" because it appears to nestle in the lap of the mountains. The entire area is crisscrossed by small streams of sparkling water running over huge worn rocks and boulders, flanked by dreamy willows and majestic cottonwoods.

The children's chests soon cleared up and they had a wonderful time exploring. During their walks, La Nell and Opal decided that the most beautiful view of all was half-way down the street from the Achalay and, in fact, several years later the two families bought that lot together. During one leisurely sightseeing drive, they took a wrong turn on the Cuadrado and ended up near Córdoba. They were stopped at a police checkpoint and one of the officers asked them if they were carrying any weapons in the car. Before La Nell could reply, the boys nodded eagerly, "We sure are!"

The officers stiffened immediately and then burst out laughing as the boys proudly showed them the wooden guns Don Schneider had whittled for them.

---

[49] Flag Mountain
[50] Square Mountain

Tanks and Soldiers

After their successful April Fool's joke on Helen Nixon, whose shocked response to being told the Good Will Center had burned down during the night was to repeat "Oh, my Lord" over and over, the Bedfords were ready to try one on Sarah T. They called her up:

"Good morning, Sarah. Guess what? The government expropriated the Seminary property."

"I KNEW it. I *knew* it!" moaned Sarah in gloomy triumph.

Like most Argentines, the Bedfords were apolitical. Many Argentines felt it wisest to keep a low profile, although strong opinions were often expressed in private. The Bedfords were too busy and, besides, as good Baptists, they believed firmly in the separation of church and state and in not using pastoral influence to sway people's opinions, while the Foreign Mission Board had a strict policy of keeping out of such matters. Nevertheless, they did not live in a vacuum. As usual, the political scene was a tumultuous one, but it did not keep them from going about their business. They arrived in Argentina during the second term of President Juan Domingo Perón, a charismatic strongman who had come to the public's attention as Minister of Labor during a military government, when he was a colonel. Afterwards, he was democratically elected and enjoyed the golden age of Argentine prosperity at the end of World War II. His immensely popular second wife Evita had died of cancer in 1952 and was venerated as a saint by the lower classes she had championed, encouraged by the State's propaganda machine. In fact, David's first grade reader said, *"Mamá me mima. Eva me ama."*[51]

---

[51] "Mommy pampers me. Eva loves me."

But now the political honeymoon was over, and Argentines were divided for and against Perón, with valid arguments on either side. Perón and Evita had indeed championed the working class and the poor, and had promoted women's rights. But they had also depleted the nation's funds, feathering their own nest generously in the process, and had managed to offend heretofore allies at opposite political extremes, the militant leftists and the Catholic Church, to say nothing of the large landowners and industrialists. Among measures that spanned the entire ideological spectrum, there had been a series of expropriations of foreign-owned property, including a choice downtown lot bought for the Central Baptist Church of Buenos Aires with money from the Jarman Fund through the Foreign Mission Board—hence Sarah T's pessimism regarding Mission property.

Things came to a head in September of 1955. Perón recognized the inevitable and "resigned" the presidency under military and popular pressure. He was granted asylum by the government of Paraguay and boarded a ship in Buenos Aires bound for Asunción up the Paraná River, which meant that he would be passing by Rosario, one of his strongholds of popular support. The new government sent an entire army division from the Capital to occupy the city.

It was Sunday afternoon, and David was spending it with the Graves and Helen Nixon, at her apartment. At one point, "Nixie" heard a commotion coming from the street. She walked down the hallway in her ground-floor apartment to the front door and returned shortly.

"The tanks are rolling in," she said.

After conferring briefly, the Graves decided to leave immediately and drop David off to avoid any chance of leaving him stranded away from home. They bundled him into their car and headed north to Avenida Pellegrini and then turned right toward the river. The Bedfords' apartment was about ten blocks from the port where Perón would disembark, if that was his intention. They were some six to eight blocks from their destination when a mounted policeman blocked their way, extending a sable in his left hand, looking for all the world like a Jacques-Louis David painting come to life. Clearly he meant for them to turn right.

Bill Graves stuck his head out the window and said, "We're taking this boy home to his parents." The policeman did not move an inch. "He lives on this street," persisted Bill. The officer's inflexible arm demanded that they turn away. Bill put his head back into the car and turned obediently to the right. He drove one block south and then turned left again. Argentine cities are built on a grid pattern, making it relatively easy to take alternative routes. Traveling parallel to Avenida Pellegrini, they reached the street that crossed the east side of the Bedfords' block and turned left again. Once more, a uniformed man stood at the corner. He stuck out his hand and ordered them to stop.

"You cannot come on this street," he informed them.

"We're just taking this boy home to his parents," replied Bill.

"Well, you can't come onto the avenue."

"His family lives right there," insisted Bill, pointing to the building. "They must be very worried. All we want to do is to get him to his parents and we'll leave."

The soldier thought it over and ordered his subordinates to search the car. Finding nothing dangerous or suspicious, they let them through. David thought it made perfect sense: the soldiers had been reasonable. He had no idea how unlikely it was for the military to be reasonable and just how dangerous it could have been. His anxious parents pulled him safely in and the Graves went on their way. They had indeed been nearly frantic about his safety after La Nell, who upon investigating the noise on the street, had been curtly told to get away from the window if she didn't want to get her head blown off.

Reactions to the coup varied widely. Through their window, the Graves saw a tangle of boys playing soccer. They were chanting, "Fútbol sí, Perón no."[52] On the other hand, Pastor Ávalos (Sarita's uncle, an avid social worker who accused most of the missionaries of never crossing Boulevard Oroño to the poor sections of town, was also a sculptor and such a contrary character that he had come to be known as "Even Ávalos" because of the number of times Ben had said, "Everyone agreed, even Ávalos!") muttered darkly, "We'll bring Perón back, and when we do, we'll get rid of everybody except Bedford and Graves!"

---

[52] "Soccer yes, Perón no."

Musical Farewell

Passengers and employees at the train station stared astonished as a large crowd burst into song. It was the entire congregation of the Distrito Sud Church singing an emotional rendition of the hymn *Nos veremos en el río*[53] at the suggestion of Raquel Chanampa's father, as they saw the Bedfords off on the initial stage of their trip back to the U.S. for their first furlough. The memory took on a bittersweet taste when they heard that Mr. Chanampa had passed away several months later, but now all was hugs and kisses. Best of all was Delia Ragni's whisper in La Nell's ear, "Don't worry—we'll be faithful!"

As they settled into their seats, they could hardly believe they were on their way. The last few days had gone by in a flash, even by Ben's usual whirlwind standards. They had been so busy and happy, and there was so much to do, especially on the various building projects, that Ben had offered to postpone their furlough, but the FMB's Executive Secretary, Dr. Cauthen, told him it would all be waiting for them when they returned, so they began making preparations.

First of all, they needed to leave Distrito Sud in good order. They encouraged the church to call their first full-time salaried pastor and put the newly paid-off parsonage to its rightful use. The congregation invited Samuel Liebert, a promising young pastor who was following in the bi-vocational steps of his father Pedro and uncle Adolfo, both pastors and high-ranking officers in a large insurance company. Samuel worked at the same firm and was poised to reach the top of the corporate ladder. It was a very big decision to renounce the financial security and social status of his lay job to become a full-time pastor. He was to become one of the

---

[53] "Shall We Gather at the River"

most outstanding preachers, writers and teachers of his generation. In one of his books he credited Ben with inspiring him to choose full-time Christian service. But now he needed six months to get ready, so Distrito Sud called Missionary Bert Coburn as interim pastor until then.

The Mission house in which the Bedfords were to live had just been finished. They moved all of their belongings into it and Sarah T. lived there until their return. Distrito Sud threw them a big going-away party on the last Saturday, at Ignacio and Teresa Loredo's house. Besides the more conventional decorations, the walls were festooned with all of the slogans Ben had thought up to generate enthusiasm during his pastorate. The words that Ben treasured the most were those of Don Vicente: "Pastor Bedford didn't just tell us how to do things—he showed us!" That night he didn't sleep at all, but stayed at his desk making sure that all of the paperwork was in order for those who would take over the various projects in which they had been involved.

Sunday morning, to the Bedfords' deep delight, José and Delia Ragni both made public professions of faith. During the previous week La Nell had told Delia, "I was so sure that you were going to make a decision on Sunday."

"I wanted to," Delia replied. "But I didn't feel anything. When I was a little girl I went to a Catholic school and when we had Communion the nuns would tell us to be still because the Lord had entered our bodies, but I never felt anything."

"You can't feel anything until you believe," countered La Nell.

An Eventful Furlough

The U.S. customs officer leaned down, picked up two-year-old Nelda and swung her up onto the luggage belt.

"Hello, sweetheart! Would you like a stick of gum?"

After several years of living among child-friendly Argentines, the Bedfords had wondered if their children were going to feel ignored during their furlough. Evidently it was not going to be a problem.

The plane trip had been exhausting. They had left from Buenos Aires and made stops in Santiago and La Paz before arriving in Lima. Between Santiago and La Paz, Ben struck up a conversation with a gentleman who turned out to be the President of Notre Dame University and offered to get him tickets to the SMU-Notre Dame football game that next fall while David rapturously accepted an invitation from the Captain to visit the cockpit. In Lima they spent the night with friends who took them sightseeing around the beautiful colonial city before the next leg of the flight to Cali, Colombia. They stayed there several days, visiting colleagues from their Seminary and language school days—the Orrs, the Smiths and the Wellmakers. Finally, they entered the U.S. via Miami. At one point, La Nell tried distracting Nelda from the tedium of waiting in line by pointing out a flag.

"That's not a flag!" the little girl exclaimed scornfully. She had waved around plenty of flags during parades in Rosario and knew perfectly well that real ones were sky blue with a white stripe in the middle.

Before going to see the first wave of relatives, the Bedfords stopped in Fort Worth. When they arrived at Amon Carter Field, there was no one there to meet them. Their ride, none other than their former Missions professor, Dr. Guy, had gone to Dallas' Love Field by mistake. The plan was for Ben to get a Master's degree in Missions while La Nell finished up her Master's in Religious Education at the Seminary. They found a house for lease, signed a one-year contract and paid the first and last months' rent in advance. The next stop was New Mexico, where they stayed with Mother Watson, and La Nell's nephew Jimmy, now a teenager, lent them his car until their brand-new blue '57 Ford was ready. They had a grand time catching up with friends and family, and showing off the children.

Ben had opted for a Master's in Missions because one year was not enough time to finish a doctorate. Even so, he had to take the Prelims, a harrowing set of exams on general knowledge that reminded him just how long it had been since he had left school. Meanwhile, La Nell ran into problems when she tried to enroll David in elementary school. He had completed half of the second grade in Argentina, but the principal was suspicious of foreign education and wanted to put him back in the first grade.

"Look," said La Nell, hanging on to her temper, "why don't you just give him a placement test?"

The principal agreed. After David had taken the test and it had been graded, the chastened school official told his mother that she could put him in whichever of the six grades she preferred.

"I would like for him to be with his age group," replied La Nell. "Let's put him in the second grade."

David was going through what La Nell liked to call "the adolescence of childhood." He walked in one day and planted himself in front of her in a scaled-down version of a belligerent teenager: "Do you know how much fun I had today? Zero!"

Nelda, on the other hand, showed her aversion to change by having to be spanked before she would wear new clothes. La Nell knew that they were over that particular hurdle the day they were in a clothes shop and her little daughter took three dresses off the rack while La Nell was having a look around. After verifying the impeccable taste of her choices, she bought them from a shocked shopkeeper.

The little girl expressed her individuality in other ways as well. At church everyone was given a small box that held a year's worth of offering envelopes. While others were content with simply taking out the corresponding envelope every week, Nelda insisted on taking the entire box with her every Sunday morning, clutching it tightly until they returned home.

By the first six weeks of the school year, everyone had pretty much settled into their new routines. Ben and David went to a weekend camp in Denton, Texas, invited by the church to which Opal Ferrell's sister Edna and brother-in-law Barney Grogan belonged. Camp Copass, located on a peninsula in Lake Lewisville, had once been known as Millionaire's Island and had housed a gambling hall and a brothel, among other things. The new name was in honor of Lady Crickett Keys Copass, who had bought the land and used it for girls' camps in the 1940s. Over time various churches built camp facilities there. One of the recreational activities was a donkey ride. When it was David's turn, the animal was startled by something and threw him off. The little boy's left arm was broken at the elbow and dangled from random bits of skin and muscle. Ben gathered his son in his arms and Barney, after calling a doctor he knew, drove them the forty miles[54] to Dallas like a madman, hoping to collect a police escort, but no one noticed his speeding.

The doctor decided against an operation and in favor of traction, in the hopes of growing a strong new connection. The parents were warned that the arm might not grow like the other one. David remained in the hospital for twenty-four days and the Bedfords had no choice but to reorganize their lives. La Nell, once again forced to drop out of school, spent the days at the hospital, Nelda with the Grogans (who rapidly progressed from acquaintances to friends to family) and Ben at school. Ben relieved La Nell in the evenings: he spent the nights with David, and she with Nelda. At first David's arm and half of his chest turned black and blue, and the specter of amputation hovered over them. However, circulation gradually improved and a new joint began to form. He was to need plenty of exercise to regain mobility once he was discharged, and

---

[54] Sixty-five kilometers

Ben spent many hours with him in the bathtub, in water as hot as they could stand, working away on that arm.

While David was still hospitalized, the Bedfords' landlord suddenly announced that the house had been sold and they would have to vacate it immediately. When they protested, they were told that their contract was not legally binding because it had only been signed by the wife, and they were forced to find new living quarters. Ben's mother joined them for a time to help with housework and babysitting.

Furlough was not just a time for missionaries to reconnect with their extended family and home culture. It was also a time for reporting to the churches that supported them and for promoting a missionary vision. Accordingly, the Bedfords had speaking engagements nearly every weekend and attended many camps and conferences. Dr. Frank Means, the new Area Secretary for the Foreign Mission Board, asked Ben to go Ridgecrest and grilled him on the situation of the Argentine Mission and Convention. They were also able to visit Myra, where they had pastored during their initial round at the Seminary, and spend some time with the McTaggarts, who were overjoyed to see their David and graciously included Nelda in their welcome as another grandchild. She convulsed them and confirmed her identity as a city girl when she wanted to help "pick" eggs.

La Nell's brothers W.L. and Tom traded churches for a semester. W.L. took classes at Southwestern while Tom looked after his congregation in California. This gave the Bedfords a chance to spend some quality time with the family's one and only redhead. He had a tremendous sense of humor and had everyone laughing uproariously at one of his jokes during a shared sandwich supper. Nelda was unable to follow but deduced that it must have something to do with the loaf of bread on the table. For weeks afterwards she would giggle helplessly whenever a package of "Mrs. Baird's Bread" was produced, which of course set everyone else off and confirmed her reasoning.

Ben took classes and wrote a Master's thesis with the catchy title of "Critique of the Argentine Mission's Work in Light of the Fundamentals Laid by Christ and Applied by the Apostles," which eventually became quite well known and widely read. He bought La Nell a beautiful gold watch in appreciation for her help. They were later to overhear Nelda explain to someone in Argentina that "she got it for typing his species." When summer arrived and school was out, the Bedfords drove to California to see the rest of the family, taking advantage of the trip to visit the Grand Canyon and Disneyland. Ben returned first on one his brother-in-law Marion's trucks so he could get in six hours of classes toward his doctorate during summer school, while La Nell, her mother and the children returned in more leisurely fashion to stay in Portales until he had finished.

Plunging Back In

"No puedo,"[55] said David sadly.

"Señora, dígale que nos conteste,"[56] his puzzled friends begged La Nell. They simply could not believe that David had forgotten his Spanish during his one-year absence and thought he was playing a bad joke on them. Within a few weeks his pent-up Spanish was released from his subconscious and he was once again bilingual.

He also recovered the full use of his left limb. After the operation he had gradually regained movement in the arm and in thumb and index, but not the other three fingers. He shrugged it off arguing that he didn't really need them anyway. His parents had gotten him an electric train set in the hopes that it would stimulate full manual dexterity, yet he managed without them, using his feet if necessary. When the right handbrake went out on his bicycle, they decided not to have it repaired. In line with the original British traffic rules, in Argentine bikes the safer rear brake is controlled from the left. David had no choice if he wanted to ride, and squeezing with his whole left hand finally got those fingers moving.

The whole family was happy to be back in Rosario and soon settled into the house Sarah T had been keeping ready for them. At first they did miss their elegant little apartment and the interesting bustle of Avenida Pelligrini, the evening visits with the neighbors on the sidewalk as they watched the world go by, and the children's playmates. However, in a short while Nelda had made friends with Mónica, a little girl her age who lived in the house at the corner, and they all learned to love their new home.

---

[55] "I can't."
[56] "Señora, make him answer."

It was strange not to be at Distrito Sud any more, even though they often saw many of their dear friends from there. Ben was area missionary, which required him to visit many different churches, so the family chose the First Baptist Church as their home base. The congregation had moved into the new educational building as soon as it was ready, shortly before their furlough, and had sold the old property to help pay for the new auditorium. Ben was immediately put on the Building Committee and La Nell was once again keeping the books for all of the construction projects. She was soon busy training Sunday School teachers and became the director of the Intermediate Department, with four classes and four teachers, as well as being on the Kindergarten Committee and Director of Vacation Bible School at the Goodwill Center.

Besides the one at the First Baptist Church, there were ongoing building projects for the Oeste, Arroyito, Echesortu, Belgrano, Redentor and Distrito Sud congregations. Ben was involved in all of these, as well as preaching several times a week in the various churches in Rosario and Santa Fe Province on Sundays, in addition to many Saturdays and different days of the week as evangelistic opportunities arose. Sometimes there were tent revivals and at others they got permission to use vacant lots, where they would set up chairs and show movies or filmstrips against a neighboring blank white wall, with a projector assigned for the purpose, usually run by young Gonzalo Pardo from Distrito Sud. Evangelistic events took place on more than three hundred days of the year, and Ben and all of the other pastors took turns speaking at them.

The Bedfords had been back about six months when Pastor Barrón came looking for Ben one Sunday after the morning service. There had been a conflict in the congregation in Redentor and he had decided to resign. Besides being in need of counseling and consolation, he wanted to warn Ben that the church planned to ask him to take over. Ben was invited to pastor the Redentor church and set about helping it to focus on reconciliation and growth. Not long after that, Don Pedro Liebert, long-time pastor of Arroyito, passed away and the church called Ben, which meant that he was now was pastoring two congregations simultaneously. He was able to be at the morning services for both because Redentor held theirs early. After a time it became clear that Arroyito had the greater need of him, and Raúl Bettín was called as pastor of Redentor.

Meanwhile, the rest of the Bedford family stayed on at the First Baptist Church and accompanied Ben periodically on his far-flung engagements. Since Ben was on the go so much, he wasn't always available to drive the family to their activities, and David learned to ride the streetcar to his RA[57] meetings. La Nell would see him on and someone from church would wait for him at the stop where he got off.

Not too long after they returned from the U.S., David announced that he wanted to be baptized. His parents had been expecting this for some time. His conversion had been quite an experience for all of them. When he was only four or five years old, still in the Beginners' class in Sunday School, instead of going to the Young People's building as they usually did during the sermon at Distrito Sud, the children had stayed in the auditorium for a revival sermon preached by Pastor Sedaca, who spoke about the dangers of having a hard heart. At the invitation, the entire shaken Beginners' class had stood up immediately, except for David, who only did so slowly at the end. When his parents asked him why he had stood up, he said he didn't want to be hard-hearted. Over the next two years they often heard him crying at night. He said he felt lost and didn't understand what to do about it, and they were powerless to comfort him. One day, in the middle of a hectic day of building and a revival that had Ben running from one place to another, he called La Nell and asked her to meet him at the church with the children, but she said, "No, come home now—David needs you." So he went home and sat down with his son to talk and pray. David finally reached understanding and acceptance. There were no more anguished questions and tears after that, just peace and steady growth.

Now that he was ready to be baptized, David went to see his pastor, Floreal Ureta, about it. Ureta told him he would have to consult the deacons. The problem was that David was only nine and at that time Baptist churches were very hesitant to baptize anyone that young. For a long time, the youngest person baptized at the First Baptist Church was Carlos Caramutti, and he had been twelve. Ureta kept putting the matter off because he knew the deacons would never agree, and David would ask him about it every few

---

[57] Royal Ambassadors, a Baptist missions organization for boys.

months. Ben offered to baptize him at Redentor but David felt he should be baptized at his own church.

While David's baptism remained at an impasse, two that were especially meaningful to the Bedfords took place. They were those of José and Delia Ragni, the first two during the inauguration of the new building. The first thing that Delia had told La Nell when they returned to Rosario was, "Now I feel Him!"

Building dedications were happening left, right and center as the construction projects were completed. The national Baptist publication *El Expositor Bautista*, reported, "On Saturday, August 30th the inauguration of the new educational plant of the Redentor Evangelical Baptist Church, located at 3759 Urquiza took place. The act began with the presence of some 500 persons. Engineer José Ragni turned the keys of the building over to the church's pastor, Mr. Benjamin Bedford, who opened the doors to the meeting hall."

Distrito Sud and the First Baptist Church dedicated their new temples during the same week in November. On Saturday the 8th it had been Distrito Sud, with an attendance of over seven hundred. Ben delivered greetings from the Argentine Baptist Mission and led the closing prayer.

On the previous Wednesday, it had been the turn of the First Baptist Church. In its April 1959 issue, *The Baptist World* reported:

> *The first persons baptized in the new sanctuary of the First Baptist Church, Rosario, were the architect and his wife, both converted during the construction of the building. More than 2,000 people were present for the opening of the auditorium, which will seat 1,000, and more than 400 were turned away.*
>
> *Located in the heart of downtown Rosario, the church was made possible by gifts from the Jarman Foundation, the Lottie Moon Christmas offering and the members themselves. More than 200,000 people live within walking distance of the building. The educational building, completed a year before the auditorium, houses a fully graded Sunday school. Eighty-five of the 250 church members are Sunday school officers and teachers.*

Baptist work in Rosario was growing by leaps and bounds. A dedicated, well-prepared and enthusiastic generation of pastors and laymen was coming of age, and the Bedfords loved being part of it. There was plenty to keep them busy there for the rest of their working lives.

A Wad of Chewing Gum

The cache of chewing gum was quite providential. Each of the six travelers worked up a respectable wad to help plug up the gas tank. This procedure, repeated several times, allowed them to conserve enough of the precious fuel to make it to the next of the far-flung filling stations. The children, who had been bouncing around like grimy corks of champagne as the Estanciera (an Argentine version of the Jeep) churned up dust and gravel, were delighted with the ingenious patch for the hole a sharp rock had made. The adults were somewhat less enthusiastic about the rustic suspension over the nearly one thousand kilometers[58] of dirt and gravel roads between Viedma and Comodoro Rivadavia.

"You can go if you want to, but I'm staying. I'm happy here: I have my friends, my church and my school. I can visit you in the summers," David had said flatly only a few weeks before.

Nelda, who had just finished pre-kindergarten, saw the look on her parents' faces and hastened to cheer them up—"I'll go with you!"

Ben asked his son, "Would you at least be willing to come with us and check it out?"

"O.K.," said David grudgingly. "I'll go look."

The conversation around the breakfast table had to do with the possibility of the family pulling up stakes and moving far down south, to Comodoro Rivadavia. It had all started during a

---

[58] Six-hundred and twenty miles

simultaneous Pastors' Conference and WMU[59] Convention, at which Ben and La Nell had each heard separately the latest news on an area that had been the subject of prayer for some time by all of the Baptist churches in Argentina.

This was Patagonia, where there was no Evangelical work, as it had been closed to any such activity while it had been a military zone. A property had been bought much earlier in Bariloche in the Río Negro Province but, by the time the building was up, permission to meet had been withdrawn. Now the area was being opened up again and the Argentine Baptist Convention, which did not have the funds to support work there at the time, had made an urgent request for an experienced missionary family to go to Comodoro Rivadavia. When they talked about it later, Ben and La Nell discovered that they had each felt deeply moved to consider the possibility. They began to pray about it and shared some of their thoughts with the children.

A trip to Comodoro was planned to get a feel for the place and help confirm whether or not it was the right thing to do. The four of them travelled around nine hundred kilometers[60] by train and bus to Bahía Blanca, in southern Buenos Aires Province, where they were met by area missionaries Charles and Bernadene Campbell. They took them the rest of the way in their tough Estanciera through scrubby terrain that appeared to be something between a desert and rough grasslands.

Patagonia is a fascinating place, but its vast semi-arid expanses and cold weather had made it unattractive to the urban-minded Spanish colonists. There were some native inhabitants, mostly tough semi-nomadic people. The colonial attitude persisted when Argentina became an independent nation in the early nineteenth century, so the government was glad to grant lands to immigrants seeking remote places in which to settle and preserve their native cultures. The first Welsh colony was established in 1865, with around two hundred persons who arrived in Puerto Madryn after an eight-week voyage in the *Mimosa*. Although the land was not the fertile paradise they had been led to expect, they eventually set up an irrigation system in the Chubut valley and developed rich farms, attracting a large number of their fellow countrymen. The British,

---

[59] Women's Missionary Union
[60] Five hundred sixty miles

who had failed in several military attempts to take over Argentina, not only played a consistently important economic role as a major buyer of agricultural products and builder of the banking and railroad industry infrastructure, but also went in for sheep farming in a big way in Patagonia, following the model that had worked so well in the Falklands and New Zealand. There were large settlements of Germans and Swiss, but mostly to the West in the Andes, whose majesty dwarfed even their native Alps.

Comodoro Rivadavia itself, named for the outstanding naval grandson of the nation's first president, was founded by decree in February of 1901 as a port for the inland settlement of Colonia Sarmiento. In 1903, six hundred Afrikaner families arrived following the defeat in the Second Boer War and settled down to farm on lands granted to them around Comodoro Rivadavia. Their biggest problem was the water shortage, which forced them to cart water to their land in ox-driven wagons. In 1907 a drilling crew searching for water struck oil. In Argentina all mineral deposits belong to the state, so the settlers were given new lands in Sarmiento and its surroundings. By 1919 there were over one thousand seven hundred oil workers living in small sheet-metal houses with no heating or electricity, facing freezing temperatures and winds blowing around one hundred kilometers[61] per hour. In 1922 the state oil company YPF[62] was created and Comodoro eventually became the "National Oil Capital." In the late 1950s the government promoted an oil development campaign and granted contracts to foreign oil companies.

After a tour that included Puerto Madryn, Trelew and Comodoro, the Bedfords flew back to Bahía Blanca in a twin-motor DC3 with only a couple of stops along the way. The whole thing had been a startling contrast to Rosario's sophisticated urban landscape and lush river-side vegetation, well-established Evangelical work and abundance of trained and capable workers, to say nothing of friends. David spoke for them all when he prayed one day, "Lord, if it is your will for us to stay in Rosario, we'll be glad to do it!"

Nevertheless, Ben and La Nell soon became convinced that they were meant to go to Comodoro, and even David finally agreed. They communicated their decision to the Mission and then to the

---

[61] Sixty miles
[62] Yacimientos Petrolíferos Fiscales (Fiscal Oil Fields)

churches in Rosario. The congregation in Arroyito was particularly affected. They had been hoping that Ben would be their pastor for a long time and do for them what they perceived that he had done for Distrito Sud. Much like David, they exclaimed, "We have been praying for someone to go to Comodoro, but we didn't mean you!"

A Latin American Conference was held in early 1959 in Buenos Aires, dedicated to planning for missionaries from the entire continent, and the Foreign Mission Board sent its Area Secretary, Dr. Frank Means, and Executive Secretary, Dr. Baker Cauthen. As President of the Mission, Ben acted as host. Dr. Cauthen, who had been a missionary to China before going to the Board, went back to Rosario with him to see some of the fruits of the Sunday School Enlargement Campaign and subsequent building projects. He preached at the First Baptist Church and Ben interpreted for him. To his delight, at the end of the service he met an elderly Chinese lady with whom he held a lively conversation in Cantonese. When he returned to Richmond, Dr. Cauthen wrote Ben and La Nell to thank them for their hospitality:

> ...I will remember for a long time the privilege of talking to the little Chinese lady in the Jarman Church. I have already shared this experience with a good many people since returning to the States. It seems that her joy reflected the deep appreciation of people across the world who come to know the gospel of Christ and the love they find in their Saviour.
>
> The Lord has richly blessed you in your work in Rosario, and I feel that the step you are taking in moving to the South to project a new work is, indeed, a great example of missionary purpose and devotion.
>
> I pray God's blessings upon you as you move ahead in the significant service that awaits.....

Patagonia

"I could have sworn I saw a kangaroo," said Ben when he came back into the dusty little hotel after tying up Fella for the night. The family's half-Dachshund, half-Pomeranian mutt Longfellow had done a splendid job of keeping the children's hands and attention full in the back seat as they carefully inched their way forward in the sturdy little Opel station wagon, often at a forty-five degree angle, with the tires on the driver's side on the crown of the road and the off-wheels in the deep ruts left by heavy trucks in the dirt and gravel.

In fact, what Ben had seen was a mara or Patagonian hare, which looks somewhat like a very large jackrabbit and runs like the wind. All of the fauna was strange and intriguing. There were guanacos from the camel family and ñandús or American ostriches, traditionally hunted by Indians and gauchos with boleadoras, a weapon with three lengths of rope ending in leather-covered balls, which are spun over the head and thrown so that they wrap around the legs of the prey. There were armadillos of all sizes, from tiny ones that fit in the palm of your hand to the giant tatú-carretas that can be up to a meter and a half[63] long and weigh as much as fifty-nine kilograms.[64]

And that was just on land. The sea was not to be outdone. Comodoro is in the center of the coast of the Golfo San Jorge, a large ocean basin opening into the Atlantic, and its waters and beaches are home to whales, sea lions and, most special of all, penguins. Its lobsters and spider crabs are famous in the international market.

---

[63] Five feet
[64] One hundred and thirty pounds

Although the average water temperature ranges between 5°C[65] and 13°C,[66] nearby Rada Tilly is the southernmost beach resort in the world, nowadays offering swimming, fishing, windsurf and scuba diving.

But the economy of the region then, as now, revolved around oil. The government had just granted licenses to five foreign oil companies (from the U.S., Canada, Germany and France) to build up the infrastructure and hasten exploitation. The timing coincided exactly with the Bedford's arrival. Ben had made a house-hunting trip on his own and had found the ideal house for sale. Although the treasurer would have liked to bump them up the list, the Mission had said no. He finally found a place to rent, with an option to purchase, on Urquiza Street, number 515 (*capicúa*,[67] the same backward or forward, considered good luck in Argentina).

A truck brought their belongings from Rosario. They decided that their elegant living- and dining-room furnishings would not survive the dust of Comodoro, so they bought some modern Scandinavian-style furniture whose squareness would have satisfied even Agatha Christie's Hercule Poirot. They had a bedroom suite made for Nelda by their trusted carpenter in Rosario and traded the small television set they had bought on furlough (but had been unable to use due to lack of reception) for a cabinet housing an excellent Telefunken record player and radio. On the way the movers made a stop in Buenos Aires to pick up a handsome master bedroom set bought from a missionary family that would not be returning. However, the house was not quite ready and the truck was not due to arrive yet, so they needed to find other accommodations for the first couple of weeks. The hotels were filled to overflowing with newly arrived oil-company employees, and the Bedfords were forced to fall back on a rather depressing boarding house, where La Nell spent most of the time in bed with a nasty flu.

Before long the family had settled into the house on Urquiza, a little over ten blocks from the beach. The location was very convenient, except in winter. The streets were at sea level downtown and began climbing immediately toward the surrounding mountains. When there was ice on the road, it was impossible to make it up the

---

[65] 41°F
[66] 56°F
[67] Palindrome

street, and it was necessary to detour past Urquiza and come back around. The house had a living-room/dining-room, kitchen and small office downstairs, with three bedrooms upstairs. The landing faced east toward downtown Comodoro and the Atlantic, and from there they could feast their eyes as the sun and the moon rose in glorious orange and magnificent silver palettes that filled the skies and were mirrored in the ocean.

The flamboyant colors of the sun were to a great degree the result of the scattering of light by dust particles floating in the air. Other manifestations of dust were not quite as romantic. It was whipped up constantly by the wind, and cleanliness was measured not by the absence of dust but rather by how thickly it covered all available surfaces. However airtight doors and windows might seem, by the time a room had been dusted and swept the farthest end was already covered by a thin new film. The wind was omnipresent. At that time there were no windbreaks. Trees were small, straggly, bare affairs, and there was no grass. The landscape was so brown that when the Bedfords went to Córdoba after a year in the South, their taxi driver was moved to pity and amazement when the children bounced out of the car, threw themselves down and kissed the ground, joyfully yelling, "*¡Pasto, pasto!*"[68] There were few wooden fences or metal roofs because a strong wind could simply rip them off. Car doors were firmly grasped when they were opened to keep them from sailing away. There was a standing joke about Comodorenses falling flat on their faces in the streets of Buenos Aires because of the angle at which they were accustomed to walk. Nelda was only allowed to play outside after her parents had checked that the wind was not strong enough to blow her away that day.

And yet the children quickly adjusted to the new climate and surroundings. They arrived shortly before the school year started in March. The next-door neighbors had a couple of boys around David's age and so did the doctor, who lived just down the street. These boys went to the Colegio Salesiano Santo Domingo Savio in Kilómetro Tres, a private technical Catholic school which was the best in the area, while David started the fourth grade at a public school, Escuela No. 142. He often walked the half-mile through a short-cut across a gully downhill from the house or nearly twice as

---

[68] "Grass, grass!"

far the long way around. In the winter he had to take a flashlight because it was dark until after 9:00. Automobile traffic was still very light and he spent a good deal of time riding his bike with a group of boys in the "Our Gang" style who lived nearby. When spring came they could go to the beach, where the tides and cold temperatures made the sand very firm and easy to ride on. It was nesting and hatching time for the penguins, which would fill the beaches and squawk and snap at the boys with their sharp beaks if they got too close as they swerved around them.

One day David rode to the *librería*[69] by himself to buy a comic book. All of the stores were local, mostly family owned and run. This one sold primarily school supplies, comics, textbooks (one fat manual per grade with all subjects, bought by the parents) and other assorted reading materials. He parked the bicycle by the window where he could keep an eye on it as he made his purchase since it was likely to disappear if left unattended. While he was paying, the gang rode up, recognized his bike and proceeded to lock the back wheel (which had a built-in circular bolt that went through the spokes and locked without a key, like a padlock) just to annoy him. He didn't have the key on him, so he was forced to walk the ten blocks home with the frame on his shoulders to keep the back wheel off the ground. He continued to ride with them, having earned their respect by taking the joke in his stride and not allowing himself to be caught out like that again.

Later Nelda started first grade at the same school, but that first year Ben drove her to kindergarten downtown, in the afternoon. Children in Argentina generally do not go to bed until after 10:00, so the older children usually attend the morning shift and the younger ones go in the afternoon, since it is considered cruel and unusual punishment to make the little ones get up early. One day the weather was particularly nasty. When it rained heavily, the dirt on the Chenque would turn into mud, slide down the hill and cover the streets and sidewalks. Ben was unable to avoid stepping in the ooze as he struggled to keep his balance while he lifted his little girl and tried to keep the door from blowing away. His foot came out, but the shoe stuck fast. When he finally reached the door, soaked and filthy, it was only to discover that class had been cancelled due to bad weather.

---

[69] Bookstore

Lunch was a finely timed affair between the two school shifts. La Nell prepared delicious meals which her family devoured appreciatively. Mother and children had come to an arrangement: she would not prepare food they disliked as long as they would eat whatever they were served when they were guests, without betraying their aversion by word or gesture. She discovered that the children lived up to their side of the bargain even in her absence. They spent several nights with a missionary family in Buenos Aires while she and Ben attended a conference. Upon their return to pick up the children, they were astonished to watch them eat breakfast.

"They are eating oatmeal?!" La Nell asked wonderingly. She knew only too well that it was a substance whose appearance and texture they privately likened to barf.

"Oh, yes. I've served them oatmeal every morning and they've eaten it all up!"

On the other side of the coin, their wholehearted approval of the food they loved encouraged her to please them. When she was very small, Nelda had sighed over a bowl of vegetables, waving her hands above it while solemnly chanting, "Abracadabra, be a cake!" The incantation worked, too, because in a very short time a delicious cake materialized.

A visitor to their home once remarked, "Every time you make a dessert your kids act as if it were a once-in-a-year treat, when I know for a fact that you bake them something nearly every day!"

Getting David ready for school was an easy matter: he simply had to slip on his *guardapolvo*[70] over his clothes in the manner of a lab coat. Nelda was another story altogether. Her uniform was the traditional white smock with buttons down the back and a pleated skirt with a sash tying into a bow at the small of the back. The catch was that she wanted it starched to the point that the bow would stand up and hold its shape all day. It also had to be very tight. She became quite good at tying her friends' bows, but when hers got loose, the only person she trusted to fix it properly was the teacher.

Both of the children took leather satchels to school, packed with *cuadernos*,[71] *libros de lectura*,[72] *cartucheras*[73] and coloring sets.

---

[70] Literally "dust protector"
[71] Notebooks
[72] Readers

All notebooks and textbooks had to be lined with colored paper, usually of a raised spider-web design, and identified with a label.

Children first learned to write in cursive, with pens. These were actually metal nibs that fit into holders and had to be dipped into a bottle that fit in a small inkwell in the middle of a wooden desk for two or in the upper right corner of individual desks, to the frustration of the left-handed. Pencils were used only for numbers and all underlining had to be in color, using a ruler. After 1961 they were allowed to use pens with cartridges, but ball-point pens were not permitted until much later. The physical infrastructure of the school may have been a bit depressing but the standard of teaching was excellent, so much so that David's sixth-grade teacher was recognized as the nation's Educator of the Year.

However, the children's first and primary educator was La Nell. Her theory was that, since Spanish was so easy to learn to read, they might feel disinclined to make the effort required to read English. Accordingly, she taught them to read before they started the first grade. She had done so with David in Rosario, and now it was Nelda's turn. She used the Calvert home-schooling system, going through all of the reading materials and picking and choosing among the rest, to such good effect that the children became avid readers and their parents were hard put to keep them supplied with enough books and magazines.

The Calvert books were ordered by mail and picked up at the post office because there was no home mail delivery. There was also no telephone and no television, and drinking water had to be boiled. Ben seldom got to eat without interruptions, since people very logically assumed that he would probably be found at home at meal times. Family evenings often consisted of playing board games or "hide-the-thimble," putting together jigsaw puzzles or reading, with a background of radio or records playing Beethoven, Brahms, Prokofiev, Bill Haley and the Comets or Pat Boone in the background.

When the weather was mild enough, there were family outings to Rada Tilly Beach, where it was sometimes possible to set up a grill using one of the large boulders that dotted the beach as a windbreak. The children could ride their bicycles and explore the caves that were strung along the shore. They had picnics on the

---

[73] Zipped school utensil holders

Chenque, tallest of the hills that surround Comodoro landward and offer a wonderful view of the city and the ocean.

Pioneers

What did "pioneer missionary work" mean? In the case of Comodoro Rivadavia, it meant starting a church completely from scratch. The Bedfords went with the blessing and prayers of the Foreign Mission Board and the Baptist churches of Argentina, but very little in the way of material aid. The Mission recommended "doing the best you can" and the Arroyito church made a bigger fuss over them going to the Patagonia than when the family had first set off from the U.S. as foreign missionaries. They made a huge map with colored strings that joined Rosario and Comodoro, and generally acted as if they were sending them off beyond the confines of civilization.

Baptists are structured along congregational lines. Each church is administratively independent and self-supporting, but many congregations voluntarily join and support local, regional and national associations for large endeavors, particularly missions. Each church names its pastor, deacons and other officers, and delegates authority to individuals, commissions or departments according to its particular needs. New churches are usually extensions of existing congregations, and become independent when they reach a certain level of both spiritual and material maturity and resources.

But in this case there were no nearby churches and the Bedfords arrived in town with only one contact. This was the Marzocchi family, Baptists from the Banfield church in the Southern Buenos Aires Metropolitan Area. There was Juan, who kept the books for the gas company, his wife Elsa and their three children: two teenage daughters, Elsita and Graciela, and a small son, Horacio. The two couples met several times for prayer and planning, and decided to hold their first "formal" meeting on Easter at the Bedfords' house, in preparation for which they took out ads in the newspaper, visited their neighbors and handed out tracts.

On Easter Sunday their number was doubled by two families that had seen their newspaper advertisement: the Véjars and the Yedros. Alfredo and Leonida Véjar were faithful Baptists from Chile who had an adopted daughter and lived on the edge of town, where they scraped out a meager living with their small shoe-repair shop and produce market. Oscar and María Yedro and their two daughters arrived looking for answers. In response to Ben's simple evangelistic message that morning Oscar, a nurse who checked patrons for lice at the public bathhouse, and his younger daughter made professions of faith, followed by María and the older daughter that night. María was burdened by a request her sister had made of her, just before she died, to make a pilgrimage to Luján,[74] and she wanted to know if she was bound by that wish. La Nell told her that the very best thing she could do for her sister was to love her children and help them come to know the Lord.

The little group decided to start having regular Bible study, worship services and prayer meetings. General meetings were held in the living room, with the furniture pushed back against the walls and folding chairs set out in rows. The Marzocchis' strong voices led the others in singing while La Nell played the piano. She began by learning a couple of hymns well and adding to her repertoire as they went along. There were four Sunday School classes and four teachers: adults with Ben in the living-room; young people with La Nell in the kitchen; older children with Juan in Ben's office; and the little ones with Elsa in Nelda's bedroom. Soon they were joined by some of their neighbors, including the next-door-neighbors' boys and Dr. Catanneo's sons. Celestina Varela began coming with her small daughter Iris, but her husband had a steadily worsening heart condition that kept him at home most of the time. Celestina told them about her teenage cousin Mercedes Pitoiset, who lived out on a sheep farm and wanted to come to the city to finish school. Her father would only allow her to go if she could find a safe place to stay. So she went to live with the Bedfords and became a treasured part of the family. By the time six months had passed the house was

---

[74] Located in the Province of Buenos Aires and home to a XVII century Basílica de Nuestra Señora del Luján, with a famous statue of the Virgin Mary.

bursting at the seams and the fledgling congregation began looking for a place to rent.

They decided on a new building one block down the hill from the Bedford's house. Besides the main room, originally intended for a shop, there was a garage beside it and a small house at the back of the property. Naturally, a Baptist church required a baptistry, and the owner agreed to build one right outside the window that stood behind the pulpit. By the time it was finished, there was a group of about fourteen ready to use it, including David, the Marzocchi girls and the Yedro family. They were among the twenty-two founding members of the Primera Iglesia Evangélica Bautista[75] because the ceremony took place at the same time as the formal constitution of the new autonomous congregation.

The regular meetings now took place in greater comfort. The Catholic bishop threatened to expel and ostracize the boys who went to the Salesian school if they continued attending the Baptist church, so their parents regretfully informed Ben that they could no longer go. A few years later this same bishop had softened his hard-line stance to the point of buying and distributing six hundred New Testaments in a modern Spanish version (*Dios llega al hombre*[76]). The "gang" still went. There were six to eight older boys captained by Luis and five or six younger boys led by his little brother. Each group answered to a distinctive call. Sometimes a soft whistle would be heard from outside the building during a meeting and one group of boys would quietly stand up and leave; another whistle would beckon the other group. During the summer, when Luis was asked if they would be at church the next Sunday, he would say, "If the weather is bad, we'll be there!" When it was warm enough, the boys would go swimming off the Rada Tilly Beach. Some time later, on one of these outings, Luis was killed diving off a rock into the ocean he loved so much.

As pastor, Ben did a lot of visiting, sometimes with La Nell, sometimes with one of the children or one of the men from the congregation. Elsa Marzocchi had a gift in this area, and she and La Nell often went together. Most people had little or no idea of what Evangelical Christians were and there were some strange ideas floating around, including a rumor that the Catholic priest and the

---

[75] First Baptist Church
[76] *Good News New Testament* (literally, "God Reaches Man")

Baptist pastor were planning to join forces and take over the city. A mechanic at a shop the women were visiting asked them, "Is it true that you baptize people in the nude and spit on the image of the Virgin Mary?" La Nell, whose attention to socially acceptable attire went so far as not using hoop earrings lest they be associated with "loose women," answered, "What do you think?" The man hung his head, abashed.

Among the regular attendees were a husband and wife whose last name was Lanza. Luis was a believer from Bolivia but Elena, a Chilean, was not yet a Christian. They went to practically all of the meetings and she grilled the leaders mercilessly on every possible angle until, exhausted, they finally said, "Elena, we've told you everything. Now it's up to you." They were working on the book of Hebrews one night at the mid-week Bible study, when Elena suddenly burst out with "I get it! I get it! Now I believe."

There was Vacation Bible School for the children in the summer time, and revivals were held periodically throughout the year, involving evangelistic meetings several nights in a row, often with guest speakers. Pasting posters on handy outdoor surfaces was a common method of announcement. One of the revivals coincided with a political campaign in which the Peronistas were papering the whole town, even pasting over the church's posters. Juan Marzocchi was not about to take that, and took the time to go back and put new posters over the ones covered up by the over-zealous political partisans. Charles Campbell preached at the very first revival and remained etched in the memory of all who attended forever, not only because of his fiery sermons. He was tall and well built, and, like many men, had a tendency to drop his full weight from a few inches when he sat. In the middle of a meeting, one of the folding chairs was unable to take it and fell flat with Charles on top. The stunned silence was broken by a bewildered "It broke!" followed by his inimitable loud, hearty and extremely contagious laugh. It took quite some time before everyone wiped their eyes and order was restored.

Ben preached at a revival held at a particularly hectic time of the year. When Wednesday night came around, he was so tired he wasn't sure he would be able to make it to the end of the service. About half-way through the sermon, six adults stood up and said, "We don't need to hear the rest. We believe." Later the Bedfords found out that the First Baptist Church of Clovis, New Mexico, Ben's home church, had dedicated the entire Wednesday service that very day to praying for their family and the work in Comodoro.

Samuel Liebert came from Rosario for another revival. Iris' father, Mr. Varela, and Nelda were among those who made professions of faith. Iris and Nelda had become best friends and were practically inseparable. They spent most of their time together: at church, at school and at home. Iris' father was bedridden a good deal of the time and her mother Celestina worked as a nurse's aide. When she had the late shift, Iris spent the night with Nelda. If Celestina was home in the afternoon, Nelda would go to the Varelas' house for "tea." This Argentine institution was a spin-off of the traditional English tea and consisted of a snack that took place at about five o'clock or as soon as the children got home from school. There were slight variations according to each family's preference: tea, coffee or yerba mate with milk to drink, and crackers, sandwiches, cookies or cake to eat. Dinner was much later. The girls were in the same class at the same school, and were even desk-mates in the first grade. La Nell had a talk with the teacher after Nelda's first report card came home with only a B[77] in conduct. She wanted to know what her daughter was doing that kept her behavior from being MB.[78] The teacher explained that Nelda and Iris talked incessantly.

"Then why don't you split them up?" asked La Nell.

"Oh, I would hate to do that. They're such good friends," gushed the teacher.

During the revival, it suddenly struck six-year-old Nelda that faith was a personal affair, not something automatic because of family or church attendance. She very simply decided to make it her own. Mr. Varela made the same decision when Pastor Liebert and Ben visited him at home during the revival week. The next Sunday he was well enough to go to church and make a public profession of faith. He wanted to be baptized but his heart condition worsened and became critical. One day Ben was summoned to the hospital urgently and held his hand at the end.

---

[77] *Bien* (Good)
[78] *Muy bien* (Very good)

"Are you sure?" asked Ben, and a soft but firm voice answered, "I'm not afraid to die: I believe."

In Argentina burials take place within twenty-four hours of death because there is no embalming, and the customary wake was held at the church. The relatives who came for the funeral wanted Iris to kiss her father's body but she refused, screaming "That's not my daddy!" She clung to her best friend and insisted that she ride with the family in the funeral home's black car that followed the hearse. It was therefore rather a traumatic experience for Nelda as well, and she developed a strong aversion to funerals.

The Seminary in Buenos Aires had a new batch of graduates to place, and the congregation in Comodoro took one in. This was María Pierga, who lived in the house at the back of the property rented by the church. The garage was converted into space for a kindergarten when the next school year started. She was joined for several months by her friend Rosa Dergaraberdián. The next-door-neighbor was a foreigner who worked for an oil company and had two small sons. The older brother was particularly fascinated by María and her habit of peppering her speech with yo,[79] a pronoun that is usually tacit. One day he shyly offered her an apple, whispering "¡Para Yo!"[80]

Meanwhile, a Pentecostal church had also opened up in Comodoro. There was a disagreement within its congregation, and twenty of its members appeared wanting to join the Baptists. Ben told them that they needed to go back to their own church and work things out. Their respective congregations had to grow by reaching new people, not by taking members from each other. The pastors became friends and colleagues. They lent each other chairs and benches for special occasions, and later on Ben was invited to preach at a revival and the inauguration of the Pentecostal church's new temple.

The rented building was a temporary home for the Baptist congregation. In 1960, one year after the Bedfords' arrival, construction was begun, first of the ground floor of the future church building and then of a parsonage. Juan Spiropoulos, a builder from Córdoba recommended by Bill Ferrel, and his family shared

[79] I
[80] "For I!"

195

the rented house with María and Rosa during the process. Ben told Bill Graves that they planned to complete the structure within a year.

"Impossible!" replied Bill. "If you pull it off, I, I.... I'll buy you a new hat."

One year later, the buildings were up and Ben was the proud owner of a new hat.

Road Hazards

On Tuesdays Ben went to the oil fields and to Caleta Olivia. When the Vejars moved there and set up their little produce store and cobbler's shop, they invited their neighbors to their home for a weekly Bible study. Every Tuesday night Mrs. Vejar would send Ben home with a gift for a different family member, perhaps a tomato for La Nell, or a peach for Nelda, or an apple for David. Sometimes the children went with him. Nelda was fascinated by María's knee-length hair and loved the chance to see guanacos and ñandús during the ride, but David's presence often proved to be a true godsend when Ben discovered that at ten years of age his son was already somewhat of a human GPS. His amazing sense of direction was especially helpful in the maze of oil-fields, where Ben visited and preached and taught, both in Spanish and English.

Since there had not been nearly enough houses available to rent for the influx of people caused by the oil boom, neighborhoods of trailers and pre-fabricated houses had sprung up all around Comodoro and General Mosconi, more commonly referred to as Kilómetro Tres, to accommodate the professionals, administrative staff and skilled workers, most of whom came from abroad. Unskilled labor was mainly subcontracted out to the local population to avoid having to pay full-time employee benefits. The Bedfords were often called upon to help out with linguistic and cultural challenges. Years later Charlie Westbrook, a missionary from Argentina who was on furlough and had a speaking engagement in Oklahoma, was approached by a woman who asked, "Do you by any chance know the Bedfords?"

"Yes, I do!" said Charlie.

"We were in Comodoro Rivadavia for a time with the oil company. We didn't go to church back then, but La Nell helped me a lot. She took me around and explained where to find things and interpreted for me. That's what got me on the road to becoming a Christian. I wish that she could know that."

Of course there were Christians among the employees of the oil companies who were looking for a church home but did not speak Spanish. Shortly after the ground floor of the new church building was dedicated, five men, representing the English-speaking groups from the five major oil companies stationed in Comodoro Rivadavia, called on Ben.

"As far as we can tell, there are only two stable institutions in this town: the Catholics and the Baptists. We'd like to talk about the possibility of having worship services and Bible study in English at your church. We also really need a school with classes in English instead of everyone having to home-school their children. Our idea is to help you build the second floor in exchange for allowing us to use the building for school during the week."

The church accepted the proposal and a new congregation began meeting in the building, consisting of believers from the Baptist, Methodist and Church of Christ denominations. Non-Baptists were associate members and the whole group got along famously. They even donated a piano for everyone to use. The English congregation held its Sunday morning worship service while the Spanish congregation was in Sunday School. Then they would switch and have Sunday School in English while the Spanish congregation had its worship service. Ben preached in both services.

The oil people contributed money for labor, as well as building materials, especially cement and steel. Gale McCord, a deacon from Oklahoma who was second-in-command in his company, was particularly enthusiastic. He helped Ben paint walls as well as lay and wax Flexiplast vinyl floors. As the second story took shape, inquiries were made concerning the school. The government granted permission to offer classes in English, as long as classes following the national curriculum were also offered in Spanish. A new missionary couple, Ernest and Martha Pippin, was assigned to Comodoro Rivadavia, largely because of Martha's background in education. By the beginning of the new school year in March of 1962, the church was able to offer all six elementary grades, in English in the morning and Spanish in the afternoon.

Ben covered a lot of ground in those days not only in and around Comodoro, but also over a much broader territory. He took the whole family to Río Gallegos, capital of Santa Cruz Province, and on down to Río Grande on the east coast of the then Territory of Tierra del Fuego. He had been invited for a week of revival meetings, baptisms, and Bible and doctrinal studies both in Spanish and English at the local Baptist church, whose building was about one and a half kilometers[81] from the hotel. It was winter and the hotel had only one heater. Management recommended leaving the doors open at night to encourage the heat to circulate. That far south, days averaged a temperature of 11°C[82] and twenty hours of daylight in the summer, but only 0°C[83] and seven hours of daylight in the winter. No taxis ventured out on the frozen dirt roads at night, forcing them to walk back from the church to the hotel, with Nelda perched on Ben's shoulders most of the way. It was a free import area in order to promote regional economic growth, and they took advantage of the opportunity to buy a set of dishes and, to their little girl's delight, a toy oven whose burners emitted sparks when the knobs were turned.

However, most of the time Ben travelled alone. While they were still in Rosario, he had agreed to cover the Córdoba and southern Buenos Aires Province areas while their respective area missionaries, the Ferrells and the Campbells, were on furlough, which involved making periodic rounds of these large regions, besides attending occasional Convention and Mission committee meetings. The children had always slept in their own beds in their own rooms, but during one of Ben's absences Nelda posed an awkward question:

"Can I sleep with you tonight, Mommy?"

"No, sweetheart. I wouldn't be able to rest. I'm only used to sleeping with Daddy."

"But, what about the first night?"

Homecomings were party time. La Nell and the children often made welcome streamers and festoons of paper chain or popcorn. In turn, Ben usually brought goodies in the green Delta canvas bag

---

[81] One mile
[82] 58°F
[83] 32°F

he had gotten on the ship when they returned from furlough. There were almost always comic books for the children—Superman and his superhero colleagues, Zorro, Little Lulu or Patoruzú—and two or three bottles of Coca Cola. Because of regional distribution agreements, Coke was not available in Comodoro, and was therefore carefully hoarded for special occasions, such as birthdays or Christmas, or as a prize for achievements or even consolation after a particularly painful shot. Often there was a doll to add to Nelda's much-loved collection and, on one memorable occasion, a large box with a fascinating drawing set for David's latest craze.

All of that time on the road meant an increased likelihood of some kind of mishap. A wheel came right off the car between Caleta Olivia and Comodoro, in other words, in the middle of nowhere, with a carful of visitors. They managed to find rides for all of them except for one pastor who stayed to help. Ben asked Juan Marzocchi to inform La Nell of the situation. A man from an oil company who was on his way to catch a plane stopped to help. He suggested packing the bearings in with grease, a supply of which he fortunately had in the trunk of his car. He rolled up his sleeves and struggled for ages to get the wheel back on. Before resuming his journey, he told Ben that he thought he would be able to make it back to Comodoro if he drove very slowly. He was right—it was almost breakfast time before he limped his way into the repair shop in town. A few months later, the family was coming down the mountain on the way back from Mission Meeting when a Jeep pulling a cart passed them. One of the wheels caught a rock and threw it up into their windshield, where the hole radiated out into a web of cracks that spread all over the glass. La Nell got into the back with the children, and they crept the rest of the way in as little bits of glass fell into Ben's lap. The mechanic put in a new windshield and gave the car a general check-up.

"You know," he told Ben, "your steering mechanism was hanging by a thread. If you had been going at a normal speed and had made any kind of a brusque maneuver, you would have sailed right off the side of the mountain."

Even more exciting was when, after a visit by the Ferrells, La Nell, Opal and three-year-old Betty took a flight out. One of the motors quit working shortly after takeoff and burst into flames. The plane barely made it back to the airport. Betty gave the episode full dramatic value with a little embellishment of her own: "And the plane crashed and we didn't die!"

Even without mechanical problems, trips "up north" to Buenos Aires or Córdoba could be very tedious given the long distances. La Nell had a brainwave to keep the children distracted over the stretches of bad road, often lasting one hundred kilometers[84] at a time, bumping along with one set of wheels on the road and the other in a rut. She took along notebooks, pencils and colors. When the bumpy part started, the children held the pencils loosely on the paper, and the jerky motion formed all sorts of abstract designs which they transformed into colorful kaleidoscopes while the road was smooth.

---

[84] Sixty miles

Camp Stories

There were two guaranteed family trips "up north" every year during the school winter and summer breaks to attend Mission Meetings. The Foreign Mission Board delegated to the local Missions the task of assigning human resources and allocating funds for projects within the country. The missionaries held committee meetings and general meetings, shared their experiences, prayed and also relaxed together, while the children played. Winter meetings were held in the new buildings of the International Baptist Seminary in Buenos Aires. Although it was mainly an Argentine institution, it also had students from Uruguay, Paraguay and Chile. The facilities, built in the Virginian neoclassical architectural style, were inaugurated in 1953, with William Cooper as the first rector. The Women's Institute in Rosario was incorporated into the Seminary that same year. Missionaries from the interior welcomed the chance to visit the Capital and enjoy its sophisticated offerings.

In the summer, however, meetings were held in the Province of Córdoba, where the Mission had a small property donated by former missionary Leroy David, in the little town of Bialet Massé. It was only a few miles from Córdoba City, nestled in the mountains within walking distance of the Cosquín River and only a few blocks from the San Roque Lake. The town was named after Juan Bialet Massé, a nationalized Spaniard who held degrees in medicine and law, and had overlapping careers as a physician, academic, entrepreneur and politician. Among his numerous projects was the building of the Dique San Roque, a dam that was the largest in the world when it was finished in 1889. Its purpose was to ensure that Córdoba City was supplied with drinking water and irrigation throughout the year, especially during the dry winter season from March to November. Bialet Massé had founded one of the first Portland cement factories in South America. He built a furnace to produce hydraulic lime. Its interior was lined with steatite and had a one hundred meter[85] tunnel for extracting the material. His company La Primera was given the contract to build the dam and the project was directed by Engineer Carlos Cassaffousth. When the railroad branch was built, materials were thrown down from the mountain sides, where they eventually obstructed the drains on the sand traps, so that the dam became nearly dry in 1892. An investigation was mounted and a report drawn up indicating ninety structural flaws in the dam and calling for repairs to be made using English cement. Bialet Massé and Cassaffousth were imprisoned for thirteen months until they were cleared of all charges. Bialet Massé sued the author of the report for the illegal exercise and use of the engineering profession. An even larger dam was built in 1944 and the old dam was dynamited, but a large part proved to be immovable and can still be seen today when the water level is low.

The Baptist Mission camp's facilities were rather rudimentary. Water had to be drawn from a well and sleeping arrangements consisted of running a wire across the middle of the meeting room and hanging sheets from it, with men on one side and women and small children on the other. The Mission looked into buying some adjacent property, and found that none of it was for sale, having been declared a military zone. The camp continued to be used for associational camps and activities, but a search began for new Mission campgrounds.

The summer before the Bedfords went to Comodoro the Mission rented a resort in Sierra de la Ventana in southeast Buenos Aires Province. One afternoon while Charles Campbell was taking advantage of the tennis courts, he overheard veteran nine-year-old David giving newcomer Wimpy Smith the following advice:

"You may never be able to speak the language like the nationals but, if you want to be a good missionary, you just have to love the people."

Bill Ferrell soon found the ideal camp grounds, in the middle of Cordoba's Punilla Valley, only a ten-minute drive from Don Schneider's inn in La Falda, in an area known as Vertientes de Thea because of its natural springs. Several lots were bought, totaling

---

[85] Three hundred thirty feet

fourteen hectares.[86] A stream, Arroyo La Higuerita,[87] bordered the property and joined the San Francisco or Grande River just outside the premises, on its way to merge with the Cosquín River and spill into the San Roque Lake. Springs ran underground and came to the surface, forming a creek at the far end of the swimming pool. They fed lush grasses and many stately trees, including some magnificent weeping willows. In short, it was a slice of heaven. The accommodations were not nearly as paradisiacal and the missionaries soon had names for the existing structures. There was *Casa Amarilla*,[88] a three-bedroom house with a picturesque well; a chicken coop; *Casa Administración*,[89] another small three-bedroom house; *Ruinas*,[90] consisting of some foundations, bits of wall and plenty of rubble; *Casa Grande*,[91] the oldest and largest of the houses; *El Tanque*,[92] a round structure housing a large water tank; and, finally, the last house to the north, quite a distance from the rest, dubbed Siberia. The first summer the Thea camp was used by the missionaries, Casa Grande had to be partitioned with a sheet in the style of the Bialet Massé camp and meetings were held at the nearby Hotel Majestic. Parts of the fields were cleared by a horse-drawn mower, and renovation and building projects got underway. Over the years there came to be thirteen buildings, including dormitories, a gymnasium and a large building with a hotel-sized kitchen and dining-room downstairs and conference rooms upstairs. There were also tennis courts, a playscape, swings, three regulation-size soccer fields and a large swimming pool.

The MKs[93] adored the place and spent the long summer days playing all sorts of games, stalking through the tall grasses, flitting through the "forest" between the chicken coop and *Administración*, climbing trees, splashing in the stream and hiding among the rubble. At night there were flickering orange swarms of fireflies hovering above the stream while the Milky Way splashed its spectacular way overhead. One of the first chores each Mission

---

[86] Nearly thirty-five acres
[87] Little Fig Tree
[88] Yellow House
[89] Administration House
[90] Ruins
[91] Big House
[92] The Tank
[93] Missionary Kids

Meeting was to cut the grass and remove the weeds from the swimming pool, thereby acquiring the first sunburn of the season. The sides were of stone, but the bottom was natural ground. When the trap was opened, the pool quickly filled with spring water that ran continuously over the lip and into the creek. It was very deep and very cold, and gave the swimmers' lips an interesting blue hue.

During the afternoon breaks and at night the parents got to play, too. There were softball, soccer, tennis, domino and card tournaments. And for those who were really and truly acculturated, there was even a *bocha* court.[94] The New Year's Eve party became a tradition, with its hilarious skits and delicious refreshments, followed by setting off firecrackers to welcome the new year.

The Mission was extended family for its members, and the adults became the MKs' honorary aunts and uncles. Anecdotes from the meetings in Buenos Aires and Córdoba soon became legion. The Bedfords had their share of these adventures.

The ringleaders in the early Mission meetings at the Seminary were the Culpepper boys, Alan and Larry, who were usually followed faithfully by Buddy Cooper and the younger Watson boys, Mike and Robert. On a short outing to check on her children, La Nell found Tommy Hollingsworth tied to a post in the volleyball court, surrounded by gleefully whooping boys busily building up a respectable mound of dried twigs with which to burn him at the stake. La Nell quickly referred the situation to the respective parents. These boys were slightly older than David and Curtis, who grew tired of being lorded over by them. They managed to get the best of them on at least one occasion that betrayed David's theological and literary bent.

"Mom," said Larry, "is it true that David Bedford can tear down the Seminary and rebuild it in three days?"

"Larry!"

One year all of the school-aged MKs joined in a secret excursion through the Seminary's clockworks, climbing over and around the giant cogs and wheels. Mercifully, there were no falls.

La Nell also witnessed the aftermath of the burning-at-the-stake incident. This took place in Bialet Massé, where she saw

[94]Italian *bocce* (bowling)

Tommy jabbing viciously at a fat tree branch with a long stick. Upon closer inspection, she found Larry Culpepper climbing as high as he could.

"Be careful, Tommy! You could hurt him."

"I don't care. I'm going to kill him!" snarled Tommy.

She tiptoed into the meeting and whispered in Mrs. Hollingworth's ear, "Marceille, I think you had better check on Tommy."

On another excursion La Nell came across a tiny trio: Nelda, flanked on either side by Danny and Charles Carroll, both brandishing long, thick sticks.

"What are you doing, boys?" asked La Nell rather nervously.

"We are protecting Nelda!" was the proud reply.

At Thea the Bedfords joined the entire Mission family in looking for Roger Garner, perhaps the most mischievous of all the MKs, who was nowhere to be seen. After a lengthy search that went so far as to drag the swimming pool, he was found sound asleep under his bed in Siberia.

There were more than a few incidents involving snakes, most of them harmless, but since there were some highly poisonous indigenous species in the region, they were always treated with respect, if not downright fear. The Bedfords and the Ferrells shared Casa Administración during many Mission Meetings. The two couples occupied a bedroom each and the tiny third bedroom, almost entirely filled up by a set of bunk beds, was for David and Curtis, while the girls slept on bedrolls under the heavy wooden table in the living room. On one occasion the girls had an uninvited reptilian guest that had evidently slithered down the chimney. On another, Opal was horrified to find a long black snake on the kitchen cabinet top. When she got up the nerve to draw nearer, she discovered it was actually her husband's belt. Most exciting of all for the children was the time the girls were returning to *Administración*. The more conservative Nelda crossed the ditch by carefully stepping on the bricks that spanned it, while adventurous Lynn nimbly jumped over, only to land on top of a snake, which must have been at least as surprised as she was. Lynn froze with fear and cried out to Nelda to pull her off. Nelda and Betty promptly burst into tears, afraid to approach and afraid to leave Lynn at the mercy of the snake. Their fathers came upon this lachrymose scene and soon set things straight.

Much to the children's chagrin, the Mission parents decided that their children's days of free roaming were over. MKs were organized by age into classes, ranging from Bible study and music to sports and arts and crafts. At first the parents took turns teaching, but eventually this task was taken over by missionary journeymen and volunteers from churches in the U.S.

In spite of everyone's good intentions, not everything was rosy in the Baptist work. By 1957, there were some serious problems in the relationship between the Mission and the national Convention. With Hugo Culpepper as President, the Mission took the initiative in organizing a Coordinating Council for the two entities, as well as a Mixed Committee for treating loans. They were "sounding boards" for identifying problems. Ben was chairman of the Council twice. It was there that the idea of a Fraternal Conference was born. One of the participants, Dr. Justice Anderson, reported on it in *The Argentine Baptist Mission—One Hundred Years of Ministry in Argentina* :[95]

> *A mixed committee of missionaries and nationals, chaired by Santiago Canclini, was to prepare the agenda and preside over the meeting. A list of issues and relational problems was prepared and discussed. Key missionaries and national leaders were selected to prepare papers on the issues, with recommendations leading to resolution and reconciliation. The proponents were urged to be frank and forthright in their papers. After each paper, a lengthy period of open discussion and debate was to be held. A Conclusions Committee was appointed to summarize the findings and prepare a Declaration to be sent back to the churches, the Convention and the Mission.*
>
> *These plans were carefully carried out, and in January 1961, a majority of the national and missionary leaders and pastors were present in Thea. They mixed and mingled, prayed and played,*

---

[95] Pages 215-216

discussed and debated for ten days under Canclini's wise guidance. The majority of the missionaries met beforehand to consider a matter which Ben Bedford, Charles Campbell, and several other more experienced missionary leaders desired to propose. They had concluded that the source of most of the relational problems was the long-time domination and direction of Baptist work by the Mission. They felt it was time for the Mission to voluntarily declare its secondary, supportive role, and to ask the national Convention to assume the direction of the Baptist denominational work in Argentina. After long discussion and prayer, the missionaries heartily approved and asked Ben Bedford to be their spokesman to communicate this during the conference. It was a momentous decision which changed the course of the Mission. It was not a decision made with regret, but with a positive affirmation of a needed change.

The conference proceeded according to schedule. All of the problems were put on the table. The papers established the pros and cons of the issues. The response of the group was surprising. There were moments of heated debate, but a gentle spirit of prayerful seeking and fraternal frankness prevailed. The great revelation for missionaries and nationals alike was the great number of misunderstandings without basis on both sides. These ghosts were revealed and dispatched as foolish barriers to cooperation. A lack of communication was seen to be the principal problem. The Conclusions Committee, wisely presided over by missionary Cecil Thompson, picked up all the ideas and recommendations. These are still available in the archives of the Mission and Convention.

Without doubt, the highlight of the conference, especially for the history of the Mission, came when Ben Bedford, in his clear but halting Spanish, expressed the desire of the Mission to turn over the leadership of the Baptist work in Argentina to the

Convention. This was a frank admission, and somewhat of a confession, that the Mission, consciously or unconsciously, had been too long in the driver's seat, paternalistically directing and subsidizing the overall work; but at the same time, it was an honest attempt to radically change its role. A profound silence of surprise fell over the meeting! After a moment, it seems that the national leaders, even the most vehement in their criticism of the Mission, believed for the first time that the Mission sincerely wanted to step back and follow the Convention as a good partner. From that moment, the Mission tried valiantly to follow the general direction of the Convention, while at the same time preserving its autonomy as an independent Baptist body responsible to its supporting entity.

To make a long story short, the conference ended on a positive note. Santiago Canclini brought a stirring message on the subject, "Let's Take the High Road and the Long Look," in which he said we should not look to the Mission nor to the Convention to direct the work, but we should look up to Jesus Christ who is the Supreme Leader. Pastors and missionaries spontaneously fell to their knees in prayer and praise to God. With tears of joy, missionaries and pastors tarried amidst hugs of reconciliation and a new resolve to work together in supranational love and cooperation. Since that time, the Mission has tried valiantly to gear all of its policy to the posture of Thea, and the Convention has strived to assume the leadership.

Of Babies and Baptisms

A sinking feeling spread over La Nell as she became aware of a peculiar taste in her mouth and, as soon as she told her husband, "Ben, I'm pregnant," he shared in her imminent sense of doom. After miscarrying yet another baby boy during their summer trip to Córdoba, they had decided to call it quits. They had been planning on a tubal ligation during their next trip to Buenos Aires. La Nell felt that she simply could not bear to go through the process again. So this time she did not get her hopes up, she did not make any plans for the baby and she did not tell her children anything until the pregnancy was well into the second trimester and she began to show.

The pregnancy was far from being the only thing going on in their lives in 1962. The congregation in Comodoro Rivadavia was growing by leaps and bounds. Finishing touches were being put on the second floor of the church building. The school opened its doors in March for the new academic year, and David and Nelda were enrolled in it to help ease the transition to the U.S. school system which they would have to make during their furlough in the second half of that year. For Nelda, who automatically rejected all things North American, the only positive aspect was the little library that grew out of donations by the English speakers, and she devoured book after book, making her first acquaintance with the mystery genre through the Hardy Boys and Bobbsey Twins.

Just as David had resisted leaving Rosario, Nelda resisted leaving Comodoro: "You go. I'll stay with Iris until you get back." The arrival of the baby was a godsend to keep her from brooding and have something to look forward to, because this time, against all odds, everything appeared to be going smoothly. At first, David wanted a brother and Nelda a sister, but when their mother pointed out that a boy would have to share a room with David and a girl would have to share a room with Nelda, they both came to the conclusion that they wouldn't mind after all if the baby was of the same gender as the sibling they already had.

A new childbirth method, developed by French physician Ferdinand Lamaze, had begun to be used in the late 1950s, and La Nell decided that it was certainly worth trying for an easier experience, so she took classes and learned breathing and relaxation techniques. The baby was due in May and they were scheduled to go to Mission Meeting in Buenos Aires in July and from there on to the U.S. All aspects of the work needed to be handed over in good order. The crown of the activities was the service planned for the first Sunday in June. Baptisms were always special, and these would be doubly so for them because they included Nelda. She had been asking to be baptized for over a year and, although her parents considered that she really did understand what she was doing, they asked her to wait because they could not allow her to do it but deny baptism to other children her age about whom they were not quite as sure. However, by now they felt that all three of the eight-year-old candidates—Nelda, Iris and Horacio—were ready.

The schedule of events was perfect on paper but practically none of it went according to plan. The baby's due date came and went. The family was kept in suspense for three long weeks. Finally, on Saturday, June 2, the great moment arrived. La Nell put her Lamaze lessons into practice until she was fully dilated and ready to go. But the baby did not come out, being well and truly stuck. The doctor was forced to perform a Cesarean section and Ben used his best powers of persuasion to be allowed into the operating room, something nearly unheard of at that time. A beautiful 3.8 kilogram[96] girl was delivered but she did not breathe. The entire staff was present, including the kidney specialist, who pushed the others aside and took over. He and his wife had lost a baby under similar circumstances and he had devoted much thought to what could have been done to save the child. After five anxious minutes of frantic work, the baby began to breathe, leaving everyone to wonder

---

[96] 8.5 lb

if there would be consequences caused by oxygen deprivation. Ben went home, woke his sleeping children with a kiss and told them they had a baby sister, Nancy Elizabeth.

Ben and the children stopped by the hospital before going to church. This was a brand new facility. Nancy was the fourth baby born there and the first girl. Dr. Romero, the ear, nose and throat specialist, and his wife had had one of those boys and the doctor teased Nelda by suggesting an arranged marriage between the babies. The baptisms were postponed several weeks and combined with Nancy's dedication. The hospital staff was invited to attend and, between their pride of ownership in the miracle baby and curiosity about Evangelical baptism, practically all accepted.

A board was placed across the steps of the baptistry so the water would not be too deep for the children. As Ben was praying with the candidates before the service, the electricity went out, adding a touch of drama. However, the power eventually returned, and the dedication of the baby, the baptisms and the Lord's Supper were wonderful. Now it was time for the Bedfords to take their leave of this special congregation, which was ready to carry on without them.

Family Reunions

The Bedford family reunited in Buenos Aires after leaving Comodoro Rivadavia by different routes. La Nell and Nancy propelled their way through the skies while Ben, David and Nelda churned up the dusty roads and gave a ride to one of the victims of a road accident that had taken place near Puerto Madryn. Both groups made a brief stop in Bahía Blanca where they were received by the Campbell family, area missionaries and dear friends. The airplane passengers were enchanted with the one-and-a-half month-old baby and begged to hold her. La Nell agreed and was soon sound asleep as the little girl was cuddled and crooned over and passed from arm to arm. Meanwhile, the hitherto reliable little Opel station wagon chose to take its leave by losing all of its brake fluid as Ben and the older children were entering the Federal Capital, stretching the fifteen-minute drive to the Seminary to well over an hour. Ben scrambled to borrow a car as soon as they arrived and dashed to the airport just in time to meet his wife and baby daughter.

The first order of business was to get the documents the baby needed for international travel. This involved not one but two sets of passports because she was a dual citizen. On the U.S. side, it meant going downtown to the Consulate with the birth certificate they had obtained in Comodoro, filing a report of birth abroad and having Nancy added to La Nell's passport. On the Argentine side, they encountered a major snag at the Policía Federal: in addition to the child's birth certificate, the parents' marriage certificate was required. The authenticated copy they had presented when they first arrived in the country had been taken from them and stuffed into the floor-to-ceiling shelving behind the counter during their first round of paperwork nine years earlier, in 1953. The government clerk muttered sullenly, "Who knows where it is by now? It would be impossible to find."

Ben politely disagreed, "Allow me, I think I remember just where it was put." Before the stunned clerk could react to this unheard-of request, Ben had whipped around behind the desk, rifled through a few folders in the wall of documents, and triumphantly flourished the precious marriage certificate. Who was the clerk to defy fate? The paperwork was concluded successfully.

That left only a quick trip to Montevideo to see La Nell's brother Tom and his family, now missionaries in Uruguay, and attending Mission Meeting in Buenos Aires before setting off on furlough. On this flight, Ben and La Nell were placed in the first row of the tourist cabin, which meant that they could hook the bassinet on the partition in front of them and at least the baby would be able to sleep in comfort. Meanwhile, David, who had always been fascinated by the different types of airplanes, gave Nelda the benefit of his knowledge concerning many of their engineering and mechanical features. Up to now he had only known the lumbering, horizontal takeoffs of the propeller-driven Curtis C36s and the DC series 3 through 7. He had seen the very first commercial jet (a DeHavilland Comet 4) land at the Comodoro airport, but this DC-8 was his first time to fly on one. It felt cavernous and, as it raced down the runway picking up speed, the front of the plane seemed to rise, an effect of the hitherto unknown acceleration on the eardrums, before nosing up in earnest and appearing to leap into the air.

The Grogans met them at the Love Field airport in Texas and, after a spirited reunion of the two families' four adults and eight children, a nice car was rented to make the drive to Clovis, where a friend with a dealership would give them a good price on a used vehicle for their stateside sojourn. Unfortunately, soon after they got under way something went haywire in the electrical circuit, causing a loud incessant buzzing throughout the entire seven-hour trip, with the exception of brief blessed periods of silence when the wiring apparently straightened out for reasons unknown.

The first item on the agenda was visiting family. Hordes of relatives descended on New Mexico. All of Ben's siblings who lived in California were there but Mary, who was recovering from kidney surgery in Los Angeles. Except for Nelda throwing up in reaction to the clouds of cigarette smoke, it was all a huge success. La Nell and the children stayed, part of the time with her sister La Wanna in Clovis and part of the time with her mother in nearby Portales, while Ben rode to California with A.T. and Sue to see Mary. It was the middle of a scorching summer and air-conditioned cars were not yet commonplace. Ira and Helen chose to drive at night, but the older brother had his own method for combating the daytime heat. This consisted of setting a bucket of ice in the middle, facing the dashboard, and turning the fan on full blast to send cool air swirling around the interior of the vehicle. During the next family reunion, Mary was unintentionally to hurt the feelings of her daughter Carla, who had recently given her parents their one and only grandson Mark, when she exclaimed upon seeing Nancy, "That is the prettiest baby I have ever seen in my life!"

Ben returned to Clovis in one of his brother-in-law Marion's trucks, napping on the cot in the cabin behind the driver's seat. Marion regularly sent trucks to California, hauling merchandise there to cover expenses, in order to stock up on fresh produce, which he kept at his warehouse, where had converted a couple of railroad cars into refrigerated units to hold the perishable goods until they were distributed to the retail stores.

Meanwhile the children got the extended family straight in their minds and basked in the attention of grandmothers, aunts, uncles and cousins. Nelda had a wonderful time with her cousin Sarah Nell, who had an amazing collection of Nancy Drew books and initiated her in the delights of playing jacks and roller-skating. Billie and Marion gave the children treats from their supermarket, and Grandmother Watson cooked up one delicious meal after another from her home garden. When Ben returned from California he made a deal on a used car, a 1957 Ford. Then it was time to go to Fort Worth, rent Seminary housing and get down to business.

Back to School

Most people imagine missionary furloughs to be leisurely vacations punctuated by occasional speaking engagements. The reality is somewhat different. In this case, the Bedfords had one year of furlough coming plus six months of paid leave that had been pending since their appointment as missionaries. The plan was for La Nell to finish her twice-postponed Master's degree and for Ben to complete his doctorate—course work, orals and dissertation—within two school years, which meant that they would be off salary for several months. Their finances would require very careful budgeting.

During the first school year they rented a three-bedroom dwelling in Seminary housing. La Nell and the children spent the summer of 1963 in Portales with Mrs. Watson while Ben stayed in Fort Worth in a guest room at the Seminary working on his dissertation. By the fall of 1963 another house belonging to the Seminary became available. The institution's policy for missionaries was to accept as payment for rent whatever the Foreign Mission Board gave them as housing allowance. But after December the Bedfords would be off salary so alternative arrangements had to be made. They cashed in an insurance policy, which years later proved to have been a blessing in disguise. Ben met with the Seminary's Business Manager to arrange a $500.00 loan for living expenses. He jokingly asked whether not getting any housing allowance from the Board meant that they would not be charged anything for rent. About twenty minutes later the Business Manager tracked Ben down to his library carrel and asked him if it was really true that he would not have any income as of December. Shortly afterwards he told Ben that he had consulted his superiors about the situation and the Seminary had decided to let them live in the house rent-free, including utilities. One week later he contacted Ben again to tell him that Mr. Richardson, a Baptist layman from Dallas, wished to help a Seminary student with $50.00 per week. The Business Manager asked if Ben would be embarrassed to accept it. But Ben was not embarrassed—he was simply grateful. At the end of the school year, the generous Mr. Richardson insisted on paying off the $500.00 loan himself. To make ends meet, Ben worked as a grader for Dr. Jack McGorman and accepted many speaking engagements, which usually included some kind of love offering. It so happened that these invitations always fell on weekends during which Ben did not have to prepare for exams or turn in papers. In this way the family scraped by until they went back on salary in June of 1964, debt-free.

All of the Bedfords went to school except for the baby, who attended day care while her mother was in class. The only one that made a fuss about it was Nelda, who cried every day for the first two months. She hated everything about fourth grade in the United States: English all day, large loopy handwriting, weird clothes, book covers that looked like they were made from paper bags, crazy upside-down division, cafeteria food, time-consuming after-school group activities in which she declined to participate and for which children inexplicably wore military-style uniforms to class, and so forth and so on. Eventually, however, she made friends with Joanie, whose father was also at the Seminary. They were in the same class at school and went to the same church. Soon they became inseparable and played together hour after hour.

Junior high (the two-year predecessor of middle school) was not a major transition for David who, after completing Argentine grammar school,[97] had just spent six months in the American-curriculum school set up in the Comodoro Rivadavia church's facilities for the children of the oil-company employees. He found his first set of teachers in Fort Worth to be more distant and less flexible and understanding than his teachers in Argentina, but after a week he was moved to the rapid-learners' class (later Honors or AP), where the teachers were significantly more agreeable, perhaps because they did not have to squander so much of their efforts on maintaining discipline. In social studies, the Civil War was presented as a conflict on states' rights, with slavery as a primarily benevolent institution. His parents soon set him right on that subject. David endured junior high as well as possible and soaked up everything

---

[97] At that time there were seven years of elementary and five years of secondary school.

there was to learn. One parents' day Ben accompanied his son to Latin class and watched him raise his hand in response to every question. But David, up to now famous for his sunny disposition, had become a teenager. Adolescence struck with a vengeance, unleashing a flood of hormones that often plunged him into dark, gloomy moods. His parents told Nelda that his sudden total indifference to her was not personal and advised her to steer clear of him. There was only one thing that could turn him around at this time: his baby sister. For when Nancy smiled and cooed at him, all irritation melted away, and he smiled back and laughed. Nancy's hair grew into long golden ringlets and her siblings speeded up her already precocious vocabulary by repeating and interpreting every sound she made as an identifiable word. Before she learned how to walk, she entertained herself in her playpen and watched TV only when the commercials came on.

Because now the family had a television set, and they learned the delights of Saturday morning cartoons and iconic series such as the Dick Van Dyke Show, Perry Mason, Gunsmoke and Bonanza. They also watched the news, sometimes the CBS Evening News with Walter Cronkite but usually the NBC Huntley-Brinkley Report that ended with the trademark "Good night, Chet. Good, night, David!" And there was no dearth of interesting events to capture their attention.

The Bedfords had arrived in the U.S. as the Civil Rights Movement was gathering momentum. It had begun in the 1950s and its non-violent techniques began to pay off in the early sixties. Activists and students challenged segregation, and television, a relatively new technology, allowed Americans to witness the often brutal response. In the fall of 1962 the Supreme Court ruled that the University of Mississippi had to admit African American student and veteran James Meredith. The governor, Ross Barrett, ordered state troopers to prevent him from entering the campus. Riots broke out and on October 11 President Kennedy ordered U.S. Marshalls in to ensure safety. In June of 1963 Alabama Governor George Wallace made a symbolic attempt to keep his inaugural promise of "segregation now, segregation tomorrow, segregation forever" by standing in the schoolhouse door of the Foster Auditorium in the University of Alabama to prevent two Black students from entering. Martin Luther King, Jr. delivered his stirring

I Have a Dream speech at the Lincoln Monument in August of 1963 during the March on Washington for Jobs and Freedom.

The space race between the Soviet Union and the United States was under way. On May 25, 1961, President Kennedy had announced before Congress that an American would land on the moon and return safely before the end of the decade. Although the Soviets started ahead with the first ICBM, the first artificial satellite in the Earth's orbit, the first animal in orbit, and the first man (Yuri Gagarin) and woman (ValentinaTereshkova) in space, the Americans began turning out one first after another: Alan Shepherd had been the first American in space with a fifteen-minute suborbital flight in May of 1961; John Glen was the first American to orbit the Earth in February of 1962; in July of 1962 the U.S. launched the first commercially useful communications satellite, followed by the first geosynchronous satellite in June of 1963. The U.S. also had the first operational navigation satellite, the first solar probe, the first weather satellite and the first object successfully retrieved from orbit.

The two superpowers were engaged in darker rivalries as well. The Bay of Pigs fiasco had taken place the year before the Bedford's furlough. This was a failed three-day military invasion of Cuba beginning on April 17, 1961 by the CIA-sponsored paramilitary group "2506 Assault Brigade," whose mission was to overthrow Fidel Castro's left-wing government. The result was to push the Cuban leader to embrace socialism fully and strengthen his nation's ties to the Soviet Union. This was the background for the Cuban Missile Crisis in October of 1962. U.S. spy planes discovered medium-range missiles which Soviet Premier Nikita Khruschev had asked Castro to install there in May. There were also photographs of Soviet long-range missiles with a 3500-kilometer[98] capability. The ExComm (Executive Committee of the National Security Council), a group of American political leaders and advisors, met several times, rarely agreeing on the best course of action. U.S.S.R. Foreign Minister Andrei Gromyko claimed that Soviet aid to Cuba was limited to help for growing crops and that the missiles were solely for defense. The ExComm suggested a "quarantine" to prevent Soviet ships from reaching the island, carefully avoiding the term "blockade," which would have been an act of war. In a televised

---

[98] 2200 miles

speech on October 22, President Kennedy demanded that the Soviets remove the missiles. Premier Khruschev ordered his nation's ships to stop in the Atlantic 1200 kilometers[99] away while Soviet submarines trailed the U.S. ships, but refused to remove the missiles and accused Kennedy of putting the world at risk of nuclear war. Khruschev offered to remove the missiles from Cuba if the U.S. promised not to invade. Kennedy clinched the deal by also secretly agreeing to remove U.S. missiles from Turkey. This particular crisis was over and war had been averted.

However, JFK was a firm believer in his predecessor Eisenhower's "Domino Theory," according to which Communism had to be contained in order to prevent its spread from country to country: "Pay any price, bear any burden, meet any hardship, support any friend ... to assure the survival and success of liberty." Charles De Gaulle advised him against involvement in Viet Nam based on France's disastrous experience in Southeast Asia, warning that the U.S. would get trapped in a "bottomless military and political swamp." But President Kennedy, surrounded by hawk advisors, followed Eisenhower's support of Diem's government in South Viet Nam. In 1961 he agreed to have the U.S. finance an increase in the size of the South Vietnamese army and to send in an extra 1000 U.S. military advisors. The latter was not made public because it violated the 1959 Geneva Agreement.

The "Strategic Hamlet" program, consisting of the forcible removal of peasants from their home villages into secure compounds, increased opposition to Diem's government in the South. U.S. reporters told the American public that the program destroyed decades if not hundreds of years of village life without consulting the persons involved. The National Liberation Front, a Vietnamese political organization born in 1960 to overthrow the South and reunite the country, increased its numbers by 300% in two years. The U.S. responded by sending more advisors and helicopters with U.S. pilots who were instructed to avoid military combat at all costs, but this proved to be impossible. In 1963 several Buddhist monks committed suicide by lighting themselves on fire in protest, a gruesome act which was broadcast on television. Diem's supporters were quoted as saying "Let them burn, and we shall clap our hands" and that they would be glad to provide them with the petrol to do it.

---

[99] 750 miles

JFK became convinced that Diem would never be able to unite South Vietnam and agreed to have the CIA initiate a program to overthrow him. South Vietnamese generals not only removed Diem from power but killed him in November of 1963.

Three weeks later, the United States was thrown into shock by the assassination of President John F. Kennedy, who was shot by a sniper during an open car drive with his wife Jacqueline and Texas Governor John Connally in Dallas. Lee Harvey Oswald was arrested approximately seventy minutes after the assassination. Two days later, as he was being escorted to a car for transport from Dallas Police Headquarters to the Dallas County Jail, he was shot and mortally wounded by Dallas nightclub owner Jack Ruby. La Nell and the children were watching the live coverage of this event on the news. They saw Vice President Lyndon B. Johnson being sworn in as the new head of state on Air Force One a few hours after the President's assassination as well as the State funeral.

There were also other types of groundbreaking news. The Bedfords watched the very first presentation of the Beatles on the Ed Sullivan Show on February 9, 1964, and heard them sing "All My Loving," "Till There Was You," "She Loves You," "She Was Just Seventeen" and "I Want to Hold Your Hand," while the girls in the audience screamed in ecstasy and the boys wished they were the ones on stage. All sorts of landmark events took place during these two years: among other things, Andy Warhol unveiled his "Campbell Soup Can" painting, a daring escape from the Alcatraz prison in San Francisco was attempted, Johnny Carson became the host of the Tonight Show, Marilyn Monroe was found dead, Betty Friedan's *The Feminine Mystique* was published and Cassius Clay (later Muhammed Ali) became the world's heavyweight boxing champion.

One Upping

"What do you mean, you don't want to do the play? We spent the night so that you could put on this production, so let's see it!" commanded La Nell, whose nerves had been tested to the limit. The Grogans' house was bursting at the seams: in addition to the hosts and the Bedfords, the Ferrell family was there, which meant six adults and eleven children. They had had a wonderful but noisy time the day before. When the Bedfords had been ready to call it a day and go home, the children had begged them to stay so that they could put the finishing touches on a play they wanted to present. Now Nelda wanted to back out, pleading a headache, something she had never had in her life. The play was performed, goodbyes were said and the return trip was finally begun.

By the time they got home, Nelda was completely listless and withdrawn into a private world of pain. She was worse instead of better after a day of rest so her parents took her to the Seminary infirmary. She was so dizzy that she could not walk alone. The doctor diagnosed sinusitis and explained that the pressure and pain are worse in children because their nasal passages and sinus cavities are smaller. For several days there was not much to be done for her except to leave her alone and be as quiet as possible. At the worse point her balance was so impaired that she could not even sit without falling over. This was the first of the biannual "sinus attacks" to which she was subject for many years, while at all other times she was perfectly healthy.

It appeared that the family was in some sort of competition to one-up each other. It had taken several weeks for everyone to settle into a routine the first semester they were in Fort Worth, and things were finally going smoothly. One evening Ben and La Nell left Nancy in the care of her siblings while they made a quick trip to the

222

supermarket. Night fell and the parents had still not returned. It seemed like forever before the door finally opened. The first thing the children noticed was that their father's left hand and forearm were encased in a white plaster cast. A woman in front of him at the store had knocked over a glass bottle and Ben had instinctively shot out his hand to catch it and prevent it from shattering and hurting someone. His wedding ring had caught on the shopping cart but the momentum was so great that a couple of bones in his hand were broken, and all of the tendons and ligaments were pulled and strained. It was the first time he had removed his ring since the wedding ceremony. The injury was not only very painful, but extremely incapacitating. Ben could not type, help with the housework or even change a diaper. La Nell had no choice but to drop out of school until the next semester to keep everything going.

In mid-spring of 1963, Mother Bedford became very ill and the doctors feared that she might be dying. The entire extended family gathered in Clovis, where she had been making her home for years with Billie at the house on Mitchell Street. At one point Ben was sitting alone with his mother, holding her hand, when she suddenly sat up and exclaimed, "Ben, Ben!" From her next words Ben could tell that she was not speaking to him but was having a vision of her late husband. Thankfully, Mrs. Bedford made a full recovery and lived on for many years.

La Nell completed her classes that semester and took the children to spend the summer with her mother in Portales, making plenty of visits to nearby Clovis to see the children's Grandma Bedford, Aunt Billie, Aunt La Wanna and cousins. When her daughter first introduced her youngest grandchild, Mrs. Watson had warned, "I won't love her: you'll just take her away." She failed completely in this resolve, so much so that, after only allowing herself to be called "Grandmother" for thirty years, she put up no objection to Nancy's re-christening her as "Mimi," a name that everyone else soon adopted. Nancy did one enchanting thing after another. She loved playing among the rainbow of flowers in her grandmother's garden and hunting for plums. She would examine the low-hanging branches, squealing with delight when she found a fruit, which she lost no time in eating, or exclaiming "Uh-oh!" if there were none.

For their part, the children were fascinated by their grandmother's little Chihuahua, who had joined the household in the hopes that she might help her mistress' asthma. Patricia was definitely a "character." She slept in bed with Mrs. Watson; had a newspaper on the floor beside the toilet and waited her turn in the hall if the bathroom was occupied; knew which day of the week it was and refused to get out of bed on Sundays because Mrs. Watson would be away at church all morning; imperiously rattled a loose cupboard door in the kitchen for service when she was hungry or thirsty; and chose to sit in a place from which she could conspicuously turn her back on whomever she was upset with at the moment. She was extremely short-tempered and fiercely protective of her mistress. However, she extended permanent family status to the Bedfords after that summer spent together.

Meanwhile, Ben was spending long hours in his carrel at the Seminary library as he worked on his dissertation, making occasional visits to his family in New Mexico. One of his fellow students arranged for Ben to lead a three-week camp in Oklahoma. David went with him and while they were there he had a tremendous growth spurt. He had grown two inches taller by the time they returned, three inches in all over the summer, and urgently needed new trousers. When he put them on, La Nell noticed that one pant leg was shorter than the other, yet when she ironed the garment, the two legs were exactly the same length. This could only mean that something was not right with David's legs or back. He had first noticed in PE that one of his knees was higher than the other. Initially he attributed it to standing on uneven ground, but the difference persisted even when it was level. In typical teenage fashion, he resorted to ignoring an unpleasant reality and keeping his fears to himself in the hopes that they would eventually go away. His parents took him to a specialist, who determined not only that David's right leg was shorter than the left, but that his hips were tilted and his spinal column deviated to the left at an unsightly angle beginning about halfway down, which explained the absence of a limp. As they went over his medical history, the doctors came to the conclusion that one of those high fevers that David had had as a baby and that had been blamed on his frequent bouts of tonsillitis had actually been a mild case of polio. It also explained why he had suddenly developed problems learning to walk as a toddler. It was decided that surgery would be required and that it would be performed at the end of the school year in order to give David plenty of time to recover.

Well into the fall semester La Nell developed double pneumonia that required extended bed rest and put paid to her formal studies. As soon as she was up and about she had plenty to do helping Ben prepare his dissertation. He wrote out the initial draft in longhand and typed it up. La Nell then produced letter-perfect copy to be transcribed by a professional typist, since dissertations had to be submitted with no erasures or corrections of any kind. This involved using two manual typewriters, one for English and Spanish, and one for Greek, because the subject was a comparison of Spanish and Greek syntax in 1 John. La Nell would type a page with the English and Spanish, leaving space for the Greek text. Then she would place the sheet in the Greek typewriter, roll the paper to the appropriate place and copy Ben's handwritten Greek. Later Ben was to say that his diploma should have had both of their names on it. La Nell gallantly put up with it all. The one thing she found hard to forgive was the night when Ben decided that it was time for Nancy to stop using a pacifier. He took it away and promptly went off to study at the library, leaving his poor wife to deal with an inconsolable baby who cried for hours.

But the worst by far was yet to come. Sorrow and grief had struck even before the Bedfords had arrived on furlough. The joy of reuniting with their families was dimmed by the absence of La Nell's nephew Jimmy, who had shared so many precious moments with them at the beginning of their journey together. While they were still in Comodoro Rivadavia, La Wanna had begun writing a letter to them during her son's operation. Although he appeared to be perfectly healthy, a heart condition had been detected which required open-heart surgery to repair a valve. Over twenty young men from their church and the nearby Air Force base were there to give blood. When the surgeons opened his heart, it was found to be much worse than expected and Jimmy died on the operating table despite their best efforts.

As they geared up for a big family Christmas celebration at the end of 1963, La Nell was surprised at the mountain of gifts for her sister's youngest child Mark. La Wanna simply said, "This Christmas Mark is getting EVERYTHING he wants." She was not feeling well. Several years before she had had a "black mole" removed from her leg. It was a melanoma and evidently the surgeon had not succeeded in excising it all. Now the cancer had spread everywhere and her deterioration was very rapid.

La Wanna was hospitalized at the Scott and White Clinic in Belton, two hundred and ten kilometers[100] from Fort Worth. On the Bedfords' second visit, she expressed two urgent concerns. One was her teenage daughter Judy, who was going through a particularly rebellious stage. La Nell told her, "Judy is going to be all right. You don't have to worry about her."

"Do you really think so?"

"Yes."

This seemed to satisfy the anxious mother. La Nell was proven right, for Judy turned into a fine woman and career missionary, serving for many years in Guadeloupe with her husband Al.

The other matter that worried La Wanna was Ben's upcoming oral examinations. Forgetting that they had studied at different institutions, she pleaded with her husband, "Herbert, tell Ben what they are going to ask him."

On one of these trips Herbert's brother was visiting from Denton and told him, "You know that this is it, so make your plans." La Wanna was flown back to Clovis in early February. Mrs. Watson and Patricia visited the Bedfords in Fort Worth in March. She received a call to hurry to her eldest daughter's side, and was with her when she passed away. The Bedfords arrived soon afterward. The entire Watson family gathered for the funeral, except for Tom, who was attending a conference in Santiago, Chile. Mrs. Poe, mother of Spanish Baptist Publishing House's Joe T. Poe, happened to be in Clovis visiting her daughter. She lived in Fort Worth and went to the same church as the Bedfords, where she cared for Nancy in the nursery. She offered to look after the little girl during the funeral service and burial, which were held simultaneously. La Wanna's husband and children attended the church service, where Ben spoke and Nelda sat with Sarah Nell. La Nell, her mother and brothers, and David attended the burial, presided over by their friend Jack Ratliff. There were large crowds at both events, for La Wanna had been a great favorite with everyone. There were many

---

[100] One hundred and thirty miles

unanswered questions. At one end of the age spectrum Mother Bedford, who attended their church and had loved her dearly, asked, "Why couldn't the Lord have taken me when I was sick and left La Wanna?"

At the other end of the spectrum, these events made a great impression on Nancy, who was not yet two at the time. Several months later, apparently out of the blue, she mused, "Aunt La Wanna is not going to walk in that house any more, is she, Mommy?"

INTERLUDE –
Return to the End of
the Earth

Dr. Jack McGorman shook his head in wonder after the graduation ceremony and said, "It's a tribute to you that you are still standing!"

Ben had turned in his dissertation before the oral examinations, something that was completely unheard of. The younger professors, who had been assistants during the first furlough, when he earned his Master's Degree, were sympathetic and had given him some sound advice. Dr. Drumwright, in particular, recommended: "When you know something just keep on talking until we stop you and use up the time. If you don't know, just give a short decisive answer." One of the first questions was on history, always a strong point for Ben, and he talked on and on until they had to beg him to stop. He had actually done it: classwork, dissertation and oral examinations in two school years. He was now Dr. Bedford!

Within the next two weeks Ben and La Nell had to have their annual physical examinations, David had to undergo surgery and they had to take their leave of their families in New Mexico.

The doctors had decided that the best option for David was to slow the growth in his longer leg so that the difference between the two limbs would not get any greater and could be compensated by an insole and a thicker heel on the shoe of the shorter right leg, thus preventing a limp and straightening his spine. In practice, this translated into driving ten large stainless steel clamps above and below the knee and over the strip of cartilage that only teenagers have near the end of their bones. Bone begins to grow at the outer tip of the cartilage and progressively narrows the strip, or epiphyseal plate. To give them an idea of the pain involved, the surgeon explained that the area beneath the kneecap was as sensitive as the eyeball. David would need to take strong painkillers and use crutches at first.

The operation was the straw that broke the camel's back for La Nell. The stress from her sister's death, the mad rush to Ben's graduation and the preparations to return to the field was topped off by David's surgery. She was feeling very poorly indeed and, after waiting for hours at the doctor's office, his examination revealed that she had a collapsed lung.

The Bedfords sold their car to meet their final expenses, and Ben's brother L.D. drove them from Fort Worth to Portales in his roomy station wagon, where David was able to stretch out his legs in the back. They said their goodbyes with feelings of regret at leaving so many loved ones behind, but eager to resume the life that had been on hold for almost two years. A train whisked them from Clovis to New Orleans so they could board the ship that would take them from the Mississippi River Delta through the Gulf of Mexico, the Caribbean Sea and the Atlantic Ocean to the mighty River Plate. They set their faces and their hearts to the South, wondering what awaited them at the other end of the earth.

AFTERWORD
by Benjamin Bedford

As I read these pages, I realize that they are not really about me and my family at all, but about our wonderful God and how he used us (unworthy, without many talents but willing to serve). When I think about how God has been carrying out His eternal plan using different people in different cultures and languages throughout the ages, I am amazed that He allowed us to have a small part. It is as if the world were a jigsaw puzzle, in which God fills in the missing parts with individuals who are willing to serve Him and to be placed in the spot He has reserved for them. For each individual, life is a series of decisions, each of which affects those that follow.

I am the youngest of eleven children. After losing two sisters this year (2014), I am the sole survivor of our family. I had the privilege of growing up in a loving Christian home. I remember my Dad as a faithful and determined Christian. Although he died when I was eight years old, I recall walking with him two miles or more to church. No matter where we lived, he always found a Baptist church to attend. My mother was a humble, dedicated Christian who was always concerned about others, especially those in need. She was a true payer warrior. When she prayed I could feel the presence of the Lord more than when I did, and wondered why I, a pastor, could not pray like she did. Later I realized that it was because she had walked with the Lord long before I was born. When she died in 1975, my wife said that she was the last person we knew of who prayed for us every day.

My first remembrance of Christian activity, as a very young child, was going with my parents to a house service in Clovis, New

Mexico. When I was five, I attended revival services for a week in a small church in Clovis. One night as we were leaving the service something occurred that I did not know about until we returned from mission service in 1991 when my brother Ira related it to me. The pastor put his hand on my head and said, "This child will be saved and will preach the Gospel in several countries." At the end of the revival, baptismal services were held in the yard in front of the chapel in a homemade metal baptistery. For the first time in my life I felt the Holy Spirit telling me that I was a sinner and needed to accept Jesus as my Savior, but I did not obey His voice until four years later.

About a year after that revival, in 1932, our family left Clovis seeking work in the cotton fields of West Texas. In 1934 we became sharecroppers on a farm a mile and half from Croton, Texas, where we began to attend Friendship Baptist Church, pastored by Jess Terry. In every service, whether regular or revival, the Holy Spirit spoke to my heart. At times I would start down the aisle, but never made it to the front. Finally one Saturday night when I was nine, my mother made me accompany her to the church service. That night God spoke to me and I felt as though the Holy Spirit was carrying me forward. I trusted Jesus, He forgave my sins, and He became my Savior. One year later I was baptized. My Sunday School teacher, Mrs. Butler, was a great influence in my life and in my growth as a Christian. Jess Terry touched my life in many ways. He preached at my father's funeral and also that of my brother Troy. He prayed for me and invited me to preach on my furloughs as long as he lived.

Two years after my father died, we returned to Clovis, New Mexico. My mother, my brother Ira and I joined the First Baptist Church, which was to be one of the greatest influences in my life. It became not only the center of our spiritual but also of our social life, the highlight of which was to go to Fox Drugstore with the youth group on Sunday night after church for fellowship and a cherry Coke that cost ten cents.

When I became a teenager, the church offered me all kinds of opportunities. Sundays and Wednesday evenings were dedicated to church activities. Pastor Barbee put great emphasis on Christian calling and his wife dedicated much time and interest to the young people of our church, many of whom felt a calling to various ministries. The pastor knew and I knew that God was calling me to preach. I am sure that on many Sundays he extended an invitation hoping that I would respond. I tried to make a deal with the Lord: if He would allow me to finish high school and college, I would serve Him as a layman and then surrender to the ministry to which He called. I found out that God does not make deals; He wants his will done when He calls. One Sunday morning I had an experience similar to my conversion; I felt that the Holy Spirit was carrying me down the aisle. That day I surrendered to do whatever, whenever and wherever He willed.

Things happened much faster than I had hoped. The pastor arranged for young preachers to speak in a variety of occasions and places. When missionary Edith Mims resigned so her salary could be applied to support a Spanish-speaking pastor for the church's Mission, she accepted a teaching position in Pleasant Hill. She suggested that the local church, which was without a pastor, invite some of the young men from the Clovis to preach. Leonard Lane and I were chosen; he preached in the morning service and I in the evening service. The next week I received a letter asking if I could possibly preach the next Sunday. I wanted to help so I went, even though this added to an already heavy load. The situation became increasingly complicated when I received another letter requesting me to preach the next Sunday. That Saturday was an unusually hard day—the butcher was sick, and I had to take his place; the cream tester had to leave early, so I had to do all of the cleaning. Deacon Gordon Smith appeared at the supermarket in the morning. When there was a break in the work, he asked if I had gotten his letter. I replied, "Yes, but I can't go because I have to work extra late. Leonard works at Penny's; maybe he can go, or perhaps Pastor Barbee can suggest someone."

I sold meat and argued with the Lord all day. He knew exactly what I was doing and that I did not have one sermon, much less two. His answer was, "I will supply what is needed." Gordon Smith must have been speaking with the Lord as well because, when he returned in the afternoon, I asked if he had found someone and he answered, "I didn't try." He had to wait for me to finish work, go home, bathe, change clothes and drive twenty miles to his house. I did preach and, at the close of the service, the church called me as pastor. I said I would have to pray a long time about it. They told me that was fine, but they would expect me to preach in the meantime. There I was, fifteen years old, still in high school, with no theological training. I did accept the church on the first Sunday of December, 1942, when I told them that I was just a boy but they had called me to a man's job, so they would have to treat me as such.

I trusted God to keep HIS PART OF THE BARGAIN. My home church licensed me as pastor and gave me an $80.00 scholarship with which I bought a 1928 Model B Ford that could make it to Pleasant Hill and back on Sundays and Wednesday nights, even on muddy roads. At the request of the church, the First Baptist of Clovis ordained me, together my friend Leonard, who had been called to pastor a nearby church. The ordination sermon was preached by Dr. E.D. Head, President of Southwestern Baptist Seminary, who was speaking at a revival in Clovis. During the revival a member of the Pleasant Hill church died and, since a number of her children were members of First Baptist in Clovis, Pastor Barbee and I shared the funeral service. On the way, Dr. Head and I rode in the same car and I took advantage of the time to look over the Scripture passage and the names in the obituary that I would have to read aloud. Realizing I was worried, Dr. Head put his arm around my shoulders and said, "Can I help?" So I read and he corrected. I did not know then what a seminary was or what it meant to be president, but I saw what it meant to be humble, and to have compassion and love. I desired to follow his example. Years later I had the privilege of studying evangelism in his class.

My part was go to school, work four hours a day Monday through Friday and eleven hours on Saturdays, and prepare two sermons and a Bible study. After five months that nearly killed me, the church offered to add $10 a week to cover what I earned at the supermarket if I would give that time to the church. I had to depend completely on God. I prayed and studied the Bible, and God answered my prayers. I saved my sermon outlines and looked at them after college and Seminary. At least they were doctrinally sound.

When I finished high school I moved to Pleasant Hill to live in the pastor's home with my mother. I was happy and it seemed that I was all set: I attended college thirty-four miles away, living in Portales during the week and going to Pleasant Hill for the services and other pastoral duties on the weekend, with many opportunities for service, such as being Associational Vacation Bible School

Director and preaching in revivals. As I look back on those years, I can see that God was preparing me for the future.

Freshman week at college changed my life forever. I do not remember what I learned that week, if anything, but I do remember the person I met on August 18, 1944, for she was to become my wife. During the four years of college I learned to depend on God for direction, support and learning. Things were going well at Pleasant Hill and I thought I would remain there at least until I finished college. However, God knew that I would need a more varied experience for my future missionary service. The First Baptist Church of Portales invited me to pastor a new work (Kennedy Heights Mission, now University Baptist Church) in Portales. Over the next eighteen months, I went through a lifetime of experiences, for I had to deal with the needy, the poor, professionals and college students, all with little equipment in a one-room building. During these months, my professor and mentor Dr. Aulick would ask me if I could arrange for someone to take my place so I could preach for him and represent the Bible Chair in different churches in the State such as Carlsbad, Hobbs and Portales, thus giving me the opportunity to speak in larger churches.

There were many other influences in our lives, including the First Baptist Church of Portales where W. E. Barnes was pastor and La Nell was member. She served for a time as church secretary and as Vacation Bible School director while I was a member and pastor of their Mission. The Barnes had a fellowship hour for young people after the evening service in their home. Both La Nell and I were active in the Baptist Student Union. This helped us both as we worked with students through the years.

La Nell and I married on April 18, 1946. Even though our busy lives had not offered much time for dating as such, we did have times to be together and to work together. We had opportunities to discuss the possibility of marriage and the fulfillment of our callings. Once when we were talking about the future, I asked if she would be willing to go if God were to call us to serve in another country. When she asked if I felt such a calling, I said not at that time but that I was open to wherever He called, and she said she felt the same. We became one in all aspects of our lives. So far, we have served our Lord together for 69 years. I thank God every day for giving me such a wonderful wife.

Just as we felt settled for the rest of our college days, another call came, this time from the church in Ranchvale. Now we had another choice and another opportunity. La Nell and I once again had to pray and seek God's direction. We had just moved from our garage apartment into a duplex nearer to the university. Ranchvale was a strong rural church, averaging an attendance of about one hundred seventy-five in Sunday School. It was a full-time position, thirty miles from Portales. La Nell lacked one year and I two in the university. It would limit our participation in student activity outside of class and require a thirty-mile drive each way Monday through Friday. Our only desire was to do God's will. He knew that we would need full-time experience on the field (including the construction of an educational building which proved to be very helpful in Argentina). So off we went to Ranchvale.

We had a great time with a multitude of opportunities for service and learning, not only in the church but also in the Association and the State Convention. The Association offered the latest development in Christian education in the Southern Baptist Convention through a series of workshops. The church had very active Brotherhood, Women's Missionary Union and youth programs, as well as an intensive visitation. Another great blessing was the contact with the young people in the fellowship hour in our home after the Sunday evening worship and continued to have contact with them through the years. It also prepared us for working with young people on the mission field.

Two years passed in a hurry, and it was decision time again. When we graduated, we had the opportunity to stay at Ranchvale, with La Nell teaching in high school and me working on a Master's degree, thus earning a little money for the seminary and the possibility of starting a family. The other choice was to go straight to the seminary.

In our experience, decision-making has usually involved three elements: circumstances, need and, most importantly, sensitivity to the leading of the Spirit. As we prayed about it, circumstances again seemed to give us direction. I was invited to pastor the Myra Baptist Church in North Texas where Dr. Woodrow Phelps, a former student of Dr. Aulick, had served while he finished his studies at Southwestern Seminary and lived in a duplex apartment across the street from Price Hall at the Seminary. Although the church position was only half-time, we were led to accept and rent the apartment. We finished our ministry at Ranchvale the last Sunday of August, 1948 and started our ministry in Myra the first Sunday in September. We went to Fort Worth on faith and both enrolled in the Seminary. During the first week, we were invited to pastor the Muenster Baptist, about five miles from Myra. We spent the next three years leading the two congregations, alternating Sundays between the two churches. I did as much pastoring as possible on weekends and in the summer, but my main responsibility was preaching. The salary from the churches was thirty-five dollars a week. Our budget required fifty dollars a week, and the difference was made up by preaching in revivals and working at Safeway, which allowed me to work as many hours as I needed during the school year and full-time in the summer.

The three years at the seminary were wonderful. We learned a lot both at school and on the church field. We made some great friends and had our first child. We also learned to walk by faith and depend on God for every need. We both felt that God was calling us to the Mission Field. It was decision time again.

It was my last semester in the seminary; I had applied for the program to earn a Doctorate in Theology, which I could do while La Nell finished her Masters' degree. We had been approached about the possibility of serving half-time as associational Missionaries for Cook County and living in Gainesville while we both worked on our graduate degrees. However, we never really considered this possibility as things moved in another direction. The Foreign Mission Board told us of the immediate need in Argentina with so many missionaries retiring and plans for advancement in progress. We already met its educational requirements and had the necessary experience. When we returned after our appointment, a letter of acceptance into the doctoral program was waiting for us. The Board offered us a six-month extension on a future furlough and the Seminary agreed to the postponement.

Before going to Argentina we were sent to Costa Rica for a year to learn Spanish, a great experience. It was not just about learning words, grammar and phrases. It was a time to learn to communicate in a new language and a new culture. I had been a pastor and a leader, but now I had to become a child again, to depend on others and learn. The year ended but our papers to enter Argentina had not arrived. Of course this was a disappointment. The Foreign Mission Board had rushed our appointment and now we had to wait. Later we would realize that it was a blessing in disguise. The extra time in Costa Rica helped my language ability and allowed us to get to know new missionaries going to Argentina, as well as others with whom I would work many years later. It also opened up our first place of service in Argentina. As we look back on all that happened in our lives, God had a plan for us. He always gave us a place of service while preparing us for the future.

Upon arriving in Argentina, we were asked, 'Do you want to send your things to Rosario or do you want to visit there first?" This was the first that we had heard about Rosario, since we had been asked to consider Buenos Aires or North Santa Fe. La Nell and I prayed about it, and we became convinced that this was the place that God had reserved for us.

So off we went to Rosario to spend six of the most wonderful years of our lives. Looking back on them, it is impossible to describe how God directed our life and how He used us in spite of our lack of experience and abilities. Serving as pastor in Distrito Sud, along with all the other duties as Associational missionary, was a real blessing. I had the opportunity to visit, preach and teach in the churches of the Association. We were able to lead the churches to improve their educational programs.

In July after arriving in Argentina, I was elected president of the River Plate Baptist Mission, which at that time included Uruguay. These were years of adjustments and growth. The Mission's treasurer went on furlough and the Mission felt that we needed to set up an office to better serve our needs. So the Mission elected me as treasurer and asked me to be administrator, set up an office and serve as missionary for two of the associations In the Buenos Aires area. I told them we would pray about it since needs had always entered into our decisions. At first I thought I should accept the invitation, but as I rode the train back to Rosario I felt that God's will was for us to stay there, and La Nell felt the same. It proved to be a wise decision, for the entire direction of our ministry would have changed.

We returned to Rosario after a busy first furlough. The next eighteen months brought many blessings, opportunities and activities. The church buildings for Distrito Sud and First Baptist were dedicated, while four other buildings were under construction. La Nell kept the books for all these projects and became more involved in Christian education, preparing materials and teachers, acting as both treasurer and secretary of the National Convention and being a member of the Convention's Christian Education Board and Executive Board, besides serving in the Women's Missionary Union at the local and national level.

I was able to dedicate more time to evangelism, discipleship, stewardship and outreach, as well as Mission and Convention activities. In evangelism, we emphasized personal work, simultaneous revivals, tent meetings using movie projectors, street meetings and tracts, among other things. Our discipleship program included not only the teaching of doctrine but also putting the teaching into practice. Stewardship emphasized giving all of oneself to God, including talents, time and money. Outreach encouraged the churches to establish new preaching points, missions and churches, all with properly trained workers.

When we returned to Rosario, we joined the First Baptist Church with the intention of being active church members while we worked on all these projects. The work in West Buenos Aires and North Santa Fe was added to my responsibilities, requiring additional travel. A few weeks later the pastor of the Redentor Baptist Church met with me and told me that the church was having problems. He had resigned and the church had called me as pastor. After much prayer, I accepted. Thus, another phase of my ministry was enlarged and became increasingly important, that of a peacemaker and problem-solver under the direction of the Holy Spirit.

I had always wanted to be in one place doing one thing, but it seemed that God had planned other things for my life. For years, Argentina had had areas that had been declared Military Zones. Certain activities were not allowed there and had prevented Baptists from establishing new churches in needed areas. When this restriction was removed, the Argentine Convention moved quickly to open a work in Comodoro Rivadavia in the Argentine Patagonia. They asked the Baptist Mission to consider sending a couple with experience to begin a work there. Both La Nell and I felt that God was asking us to consider the request.

The work in Rosario was being blessed by God in an unusual way. Our family had so many opportunities for service that we could not respond to all of them. It did not seem logical for us to leave Rosario at that time. I thought of Philip, enjoying the fruits of a great revival in Samaria when God ask him to leave and go to a desert area to witness to one man. The truth was that we would have chosen to stay in Rosario, but we were convinced that we were following God's will.

Thus, a new and very different phase of our missionary career had begun, church planting in an unreached area. The question at hand was how to begin. When we asked the Mission and Convention for advice, the answer was, "We have confidence in you: just trust in the Lord, and we will be praying for you." It was good advice, so that is exactly what we did. We studied the cultural makeup of the city, the access people had for Christian worship and their spiritual needs. Three years later there was a flourishing congregation, a church building and a school. It was time for our second furlough and we were not ready to leave our beloved Comodoro. We felt it had been a real privilege to participate in the beginning of the work there and in the future vision of opening works throughout the Patagonia.

After an extended two-year furlough we traveled back to Argentina in 1964 to continue our mission work as God led us. We did not return to the South because the Mission decided that, in light of overall needs, only one couple should remain in Comodoro. We felt led to accept the invitation of the South Zone of the Greater Buenos Aires, an area of about four million people, as associational missionaries with an emphasis on strengthening the churches and beginning new works. The work in Rosario had consisted basically of directing missions and pastoral work. In Comodoro Rivadavia it had been planting a new work in a pioneer area and laying the base for other new works. Our new task was a combination of all of the above and would lead into new and unexpected areas, which will be the subject of a second book.

I have shared these experiences in detail so you can see how I had to learn to obey and depend on God for everything at that time and until today. I realize that my ministry has been in different places, in different phases, filling different roles, but always the same, whether pastoring, preaching, teaching, doing evangelistic work person-to-person or preaching in revivals, or carrying out administrative responsibilities, all for the glory of my Savior.

Everyone's life is a series of decisions, each of which affects those that follow. The most important one is to accept or reject Jesus as Savior and Lord and to put the kingdom of God above all else. I have told you how I was saved and called by God to be a preacher and how He has guided me by His Holy Spirit through the years in the hope that my testimony might help you or someone you know to become a Christian and do whatever He leads you to do.

The greatest thing we can do is believe in His Son as our Lord and Savior, die to ourselves and commit our lives to Him in service with the result of receiving abundant and eternal life, the promise to be like Him and to be a part of His eternal kingdom. It is our privilege and honor to worship and adore Him, giving all the glory and honor due to His Holy Name!

Nelda Bedford Gaydou was born in Argentina and raised there by missionary parents from the U.S. As a child she lived in Rosario, Comodoro Rivadavia and Buenos Aires. She went to college in the U.S. and earned degrees from Baylor University and the University of Texas at Austin. Her adult years have been divided between the U.S. and Argentina. Since 1996 she has been living in the central mountains of Córdoba.

Nelda and her husband share a beautiful view with their three Labrador Retrievers, only blocks away from their two youngest children and four grandchildren, while their firstborn represents the family in Texas. Nelda exercises her love of teaching in her local church and works as a translator in English, Spanish, French and Italian.

Nelda is currently writing the second book of the Bedford biography, *From Sea to Sea: River Plate to Lake Michigan*, which covers from 1964 to the present.

www.ingramcontent.com/pod-product-compliance
Lightning Source LLC
Chambersburg PA
CBHW031128090426
42738CB00008B/1016